United States Department of Agriculture

Integrating Fine-scale Soil Data into Species Distribution Models:
Preparing Soil Survey Geographic (SSURGO) Data from Multiple Counties

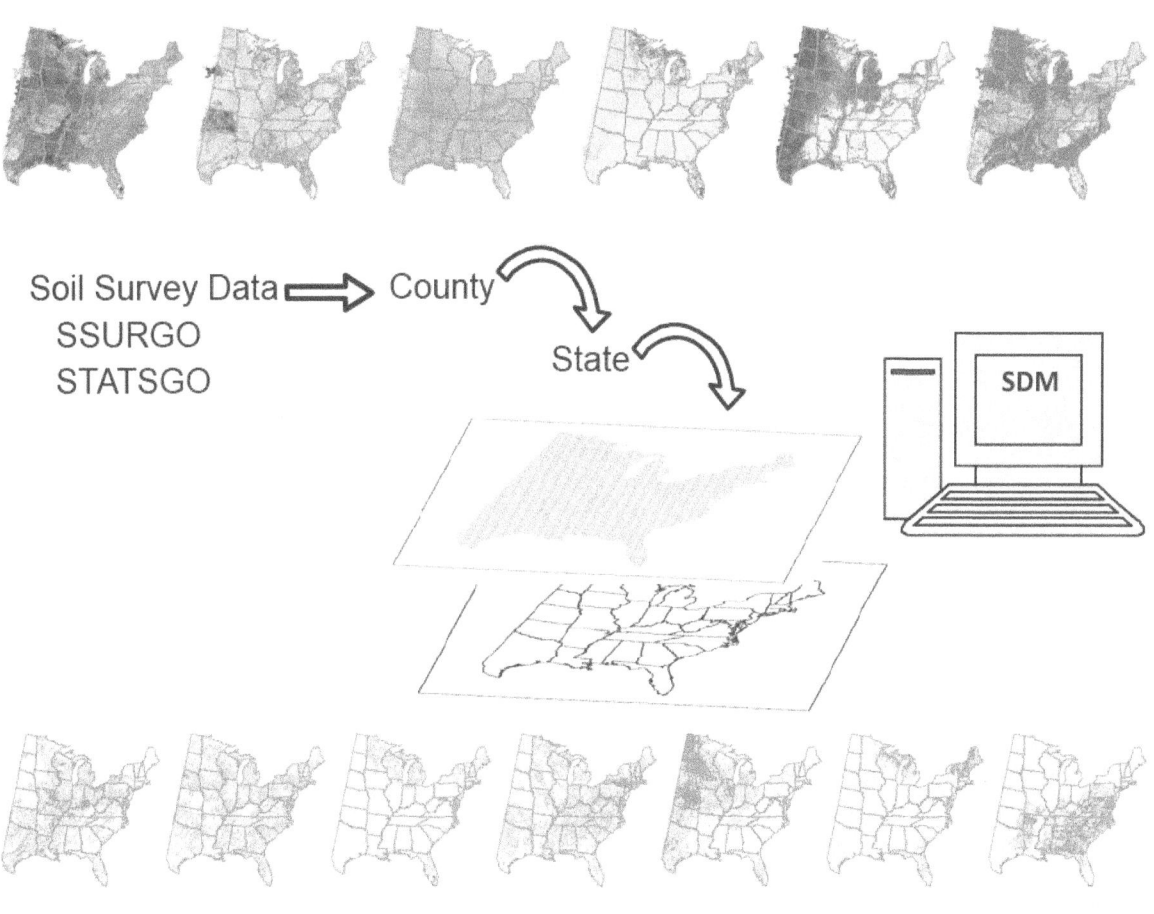

Forest
Service

Northern
Research Station

General Technical
Report NRS-122

November 2013

Abstract

Fine-scale soil (SSURGO) data were processed at the county level for 37 states within the eastern United States, initially for use as predictor variables in a species distribution model called DISTRIB II. Values from county polygon files converted into a continuous 30-m raster grid were aggregated to 4-km cells and integrated with other environmental and site condition values for use in the DISTRIB II model. In an effort to improve the prediction accuracy of DISTRIB II over our earlier version of DISTRIB, fine-scale soil attributes replaced those derived from coarse-scale soil (STATSGO) data. The methods used to prepare and process the SSURGO data are described and geoprocessing scripts are provided.

Manuscript received for publication 5 May 2013

Published by:
U.S. FOREST SERVICE
11 CAMPUS BLVD SUITE 200
NEWTOWN SQUARE PA 19073

November 2013

For additional copies:
U.S. Forest Service
Publications Distribution
359 Main Road
Delaware, OH 43015-8640
Fax: (740)368-0152
Email: nrspubs@fs.fed.us

Visit our homepage at: **http://www.nrs.fs.fed.us/**

Integrating Fine-scale Soil Data into Species Distribution Models: Preparing Soil Survey Geographic (SSURGO) Data from Multiple Counties

Matthew P. Peters, Louis R. Iverson,
Anantha M. Prasad, and Steve N. Matthews

*MATTHEW P. PETERS is a geographic information system technician,
LOUIS R. IVERSON is a landscape ecologist, and ANANTHA M. PRASAD
is a research ecologist with the U.S. Forest Service, Northern Research
Station, Delaware, Ohio. STEVE N. MATTHEWS is an ecologist with the U.S.
Forest Service, Northern Research Station, Delaware, Ohio, and a research
assistant professor at the Ohio State University, School of Environment and
Natural Resources, Columbus, Ohio. Matthew Peters is the corresponding
author: to contact, email MatthewPeters@fs.fed.us or call 740-368-0090.*

General Technical Report NRS-122
November 2013

Contents

INTRODUCTION

Forests of the eastern United States are diverse, but presence of individual species is often limited locally by environmental conditions including climate, land use, and soil properties. Both climate and land use can change more rapidly than soil properties; thus it is important for species distribution models (SDMs) identifying current and future potential suitable habitat to consider soil characteristics. Having modeled tree and bird habitat since the early 1990s (Iverson et al. 2011), our group has learned that climate variables alone may not reliably predict habitat suitable for a tree species. By the end of a simulation, climatic indicators of an area may become suitable for a tree species; however, if the soil properties are not associated with the species, establishment and survival will remain difficult. Therefore we have advocated that SDMs include more than just climate variables to model potential suitable habitats.

This report describes the processes used to incorporate either fine-scale Soil Survey Geographic (SSURGO) data or coarse-scale State Soil Geographic (STATSGO) data, where fine-scale data were not available, over a large extent into an SDM. These methods have been applied to all counties in 37 states east of the 100th meridian to process 12 soil characteristics and properties for the DISTRIB modeling framework (Prasad et al. 2006). An atlas based on the DISTRIB model simulations using STATSGO data contained potential suitable habitat at the county level for 80 tree species (Iverson et al. 1999). In a second version, available online at www.nrs. fs.fed.us/atlas, 20-km grid cells replaced county boundaries and the species list was increased to 134 tree species (Prasad et al. 2007). In the next version of the atlas, efforts are underway to move to a 4-km grid cell and replace STATSGO with SSURGO data.

Improvements to the DISTRIB modeling approach have included redefining the list of predictor variables and incorporating more reliable general circulation models (GCMs) of future climate scenarios, refining the spatial resolution of model outputs, and integrating modification factors (Matthews et al. 2011) based on species' life history and physiology to better interpret the model results. Although these improvements have increased our confidence in the simulations, there remain two limiting factors related to the final resolution: the spatial distribution and density of forest monitoring plots and the resolution of available downscaled GCMs. With the use of SSURGO data, soil becomes less of a limiting factor because these data are generated at a scale of 1:24,000 and provided as vector shapefiles.

This report aims to help those preparing soil data for spatial modeling by describing the SSURGO soil data, providing an overview of how soil attributes can be generated with the Soil Data Viewer, and discussing how to automate geoprocessing of the soil data within a geographic information system (GIS). Knowledge of GIS processes and to some degree computer programming is recommended before undertaking a project similar to the examples provided here. This report should be used as a starting point, as individual projects may require a different approach or additional processes to prepare the data for other models. Additionally, the methods presented can be used to process other fine-scale data sets provided in small sections for large regions.

DATA SOURCES AND TOOLS

The U.S. Department of Agriculture (USDA), Natural Resources Conservation Service (NRCS) collects and maintains soil survey records for every county in the United States. According to its Web site, "soil surveys provide an orderly, on-the-ground, scientific inventory of soil resources that includes maps showing the locations and extent of soils, data about the physical and chemical properties of those soils, and information derived from that data about potentialities and problems of use on each kind of soil in sufficient detail to meet all reasonable needs for farmers, agricultural technicians, community planners, engineers, and scientists in planning and transferring the findings of research and experience to specific land areas… Soil surveys also provide a basis to help predict the effect of global climate change on worldwide agricultural production and other land-dependent processes" (NRCS 2011b). Two products are offered online: a coarse state-level data set (STATSGO, 1:250,000) and a fine-scale county-level data set (SSURGO, 1:12,000 or 1:24,000) (available at http://soildatamart.nrcs.usda.gov/). Each product is provided as a digital vector file that can be loaded into a GIS for further analysis or processing. Alternatively, as of 2010, data files for multiple counties can be obtained from the NRCS Geospatial Data Gateway (available at http://datagateway.nrcs.usda.gov/GDGHome.aspx).

The newest version of our climate change tree atlas will have a finer resolution as a result of downscaled GCM data, so we decided to incorporate SSURGO soil data instead of the previously used STATSGO data to refine the soil predictor variables. Use of the SSURGO data removes much of the generalization within the STATSGO data by defining smaller polygons, or map units, for distinct soil groups (fig. 1).

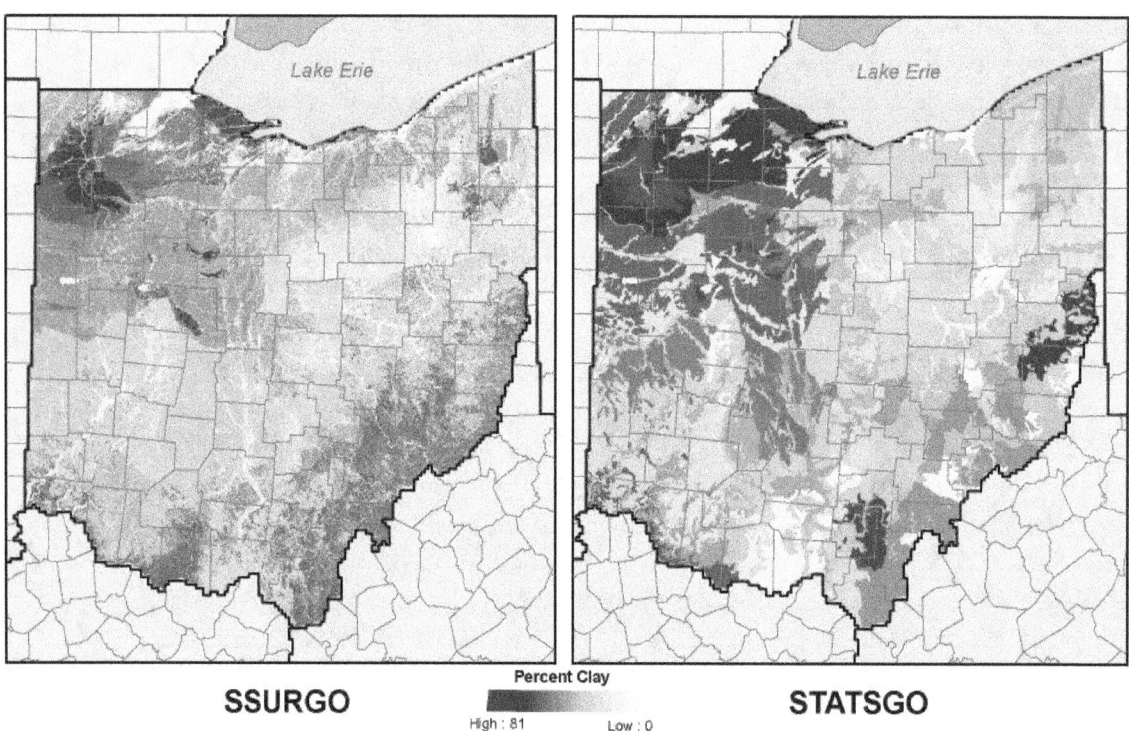

Figure 1.—A visual comparison of 30-m rasterized soil clay percentages from SSURGO and STATSGO soil data for Ohio.

Soil Data Viewer

In addition to providing soil data, the NRCS offers software (Soil Data Viewer, SDV) to aid in mapping various attributes and records within a county's or state's database (NRCS 2008). The SDV can be used as a stand-alone program to generate tabular reports or as a plug-in to ArcMap™ 8.3 – 10.x (ESRI®, Redlands, CA) to generate shapefiles from soil attributes. Although this tool is useful for mapping common soil attributes (i.e., those included within the SDV), there may be instances when values are contained in the tabular database, but an option doesn't exist within the SDV to map the data. In these few cases, the records can be exported from the database and joined to the county's or state's map units shapefile. This process is described later.

Python Scripts

Because a large amount of data had to be processed, and the processes were the same for each file, Python scripts that called the ArcGIS™ geoprocessor were created to automate much of the workload. A script was written to handle each of the following cases: (1) the soil variable shapefile was generated from the SDV; and (2) the variable couldn't be generated from the SDV, but the values were contained in the soil database. Even though automation reduced the user's interaction with these processes, a considerable amount of time elapsed (several days) as the geoprocessor was run via Python scripts for each state. The overhead from the ArcGIS geoprocessor was found to be high for these processes, so we reverted to the older but more streamlined software available via ArcInfo™ Workstation (ESRI). We found that an ArcInfo Arc Macro Language (AML) script decreased the runtime of these processes. Further details on the use of both scripting languages are given in the discussion section.

ArcGIS Model Builder

Two ArcGIS models were developed, one to post-process each of the 12 soil variables (table 1) once every county was mosaicked into a state, and each state was mosaicked together to form the eastern U.S. coverage, and another to calculate summary statistics at 4-km grid cells. Post-processing included conditional statements to fill gaps within the SSURGO coverage with coarser STATSGO soil data, so that in the resulting coverage, "No Data" values occurred only

Table 1.—Soil properties used as predictor variables for potential suitable habitat obtained from SSURGO and STATSGO data

Variable code	Variable name	Description
AWS	Available Water Supply	Maximum soil moisture (cm, to 152 cm)
BD	Bulk Density	Mass of dried soil per unit of bulk volume
CLAY	Clay	Percent clay (<0.002 mm)
FPROD*	Productivity	Potential soil productivity (ft^3/acre/year)
KFFACT	K Factor	Soil erodibility factor, rock fragment free
OM	Organic Matter	Organic matter content (% by weight)
KSAT	Permeability	Soil permeability rate (cm/hr)
PH	pH	Degree of acidity or alkalinity
ROCKDEP	Rock Depth	Depth to bedrock (cm)
NO10*	Sieve 10	Percentage of soil passing sieve no. 10 (coarse)
NO200*	Sieve 200	Percentage of soil passing sieve no. 200 (fine)
TAX*	Taxonomic Order	Major soil classes

*Not generated from Soil Data Viewer; table extracted from database and joined to map unit shapefile.

if both SSURGO and STATSGO values were missing. Summary statistics were calculated by running a zonal statistics tool for 56 groups of 4-km cells. We needed to iteratively process 56 zones containing ~10,000 records because dividing the eastern United States into 4-km grids required 525,000 cells—well over the limit that the "Zonal Statistics to Table" tool can handle.

METHODS

Computer Requirements

To process NRCS soil data and create individual coverages, the following minimum computer resources are required:

- A computer running Windows XP or Windows 7 (required by SDV)[1]
- A considerable amount of hard disk space (250 gigabytes are suggested)
- Microsoft (MS) Access 2000 (if using 2003 or above, you'll need a way to convert comma-separated value [CSV] files to DBF format)
- ESRI ArcGIS Desktop 8.3 (versions 9.2 and 9.3 were used to process data)
- ESRI ArcInfo Workstation 8.0 (versions 9.2 and 9.3 were used to process data)
- Soil Data Viewer (available at http://soils.usda.gov/sdv/download.html)

Other software that is not required but may be helpful includes:

- A text editor (TextPad or Notepad ++)
- R statistical computing software, including library "foreign" (available at www.R-project.org)

Data Preparation

At this point it will be assumed that you have obtained all soil data that you will process and the files have been uncompressed. We obtained available SSURGO files for all counties with spatial and tabular data for 37 states within the eastern United States (NRCS 2009). Each county folder contains two folders, one for GIS data ("spatial") and the other for the database files ("tabular") and several metadata files. The MS Access database is a blank template, meaning that the NRCS structure is provided without any soil information, and the database may be state specific. The soil information is contained in the text (TXT) files within the tabular folder. To import this information into the MS Access database, open the database and copy the tabular folder's file path into the dialog box in the SSURGO Import form (fig. 2). All of the database files for a region (i.e., state) should be prepared before generating the soil characteristic/property shapefiles from the SDV. Figure 3 is a schematic of the processes used to prepare the county soil data and create a multi-county coverage.

Using the Soil Data Viewer

First, the SDV software and the plug-in extension for ArcGIS should be properly installed. The SDV can be used as a stand-alone program, or as an extension to ArcGIS. As a stand-alone

---

[1]According to the NRCS Soil Data Viewer Web site, Soil Data Viewer 6.0 is certified only for Windows XP Professional or Windows 7 Professional x64 with ArcGIS 10.

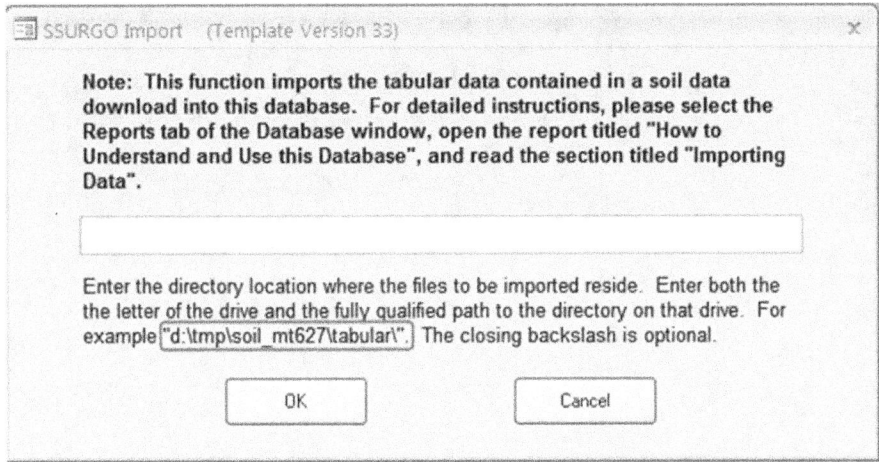

Figure 2.—Soil database import information dialog box.

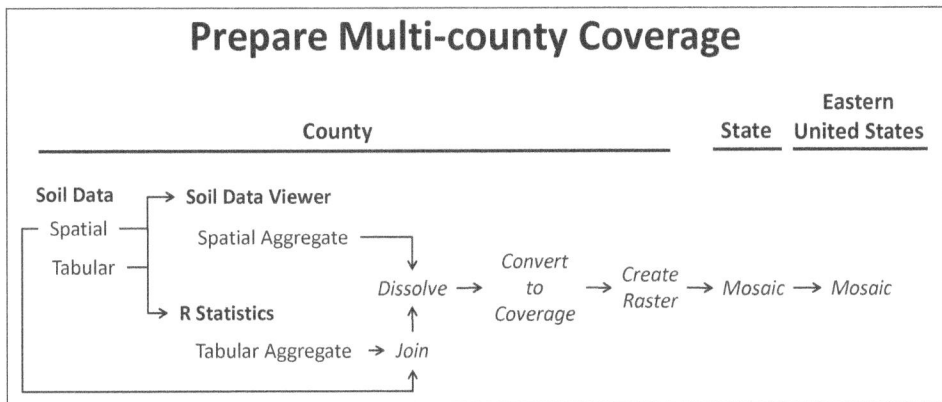

Figure 3.—Schematic showing the processes used to prepare soil data and generate a multi-county coverage.

program, the SDV can generate tabular reports only for selected soil records and attributes. As an extension, the SDV has the option to join attributes of all records or a subset of records to the spatial map units layer displayed in ArcGIS. Once mapped, these attributes can be exported and saved as a permanent shapefile. Refer to the user guide for specific issues related to the operation of the program (available at http://soils.usda.gov/sdv/userguide.html).

To start the ArcGIS extension, with ArcMap open add the county/counties map units shapefile(s) to the data frame (soilmu_a_ST000.shp), where ST is the abbreviated state name and 000 corresponds to the three-digit county FIPS code.[2] Once one or more shapefiles of map units have been loaded into ArcMap, the SDV can be opened by clicking on the ⚙ icon. If the icon is not present, load the toolbar by right-clicking in an open space of the toolbar area and selecting the "Soil Data Viewer Tools." Once open, the SDV will prompt you to identify a soil database, which should correspond to the soil map units you wish to use.

---

[2]As a result of the NRCS mapping effort, some counties have been split into smaller sections or several counties may have been aggregated into a single unit; in these situations the 000 FIPS code is reported as 500 and 600, respectively.

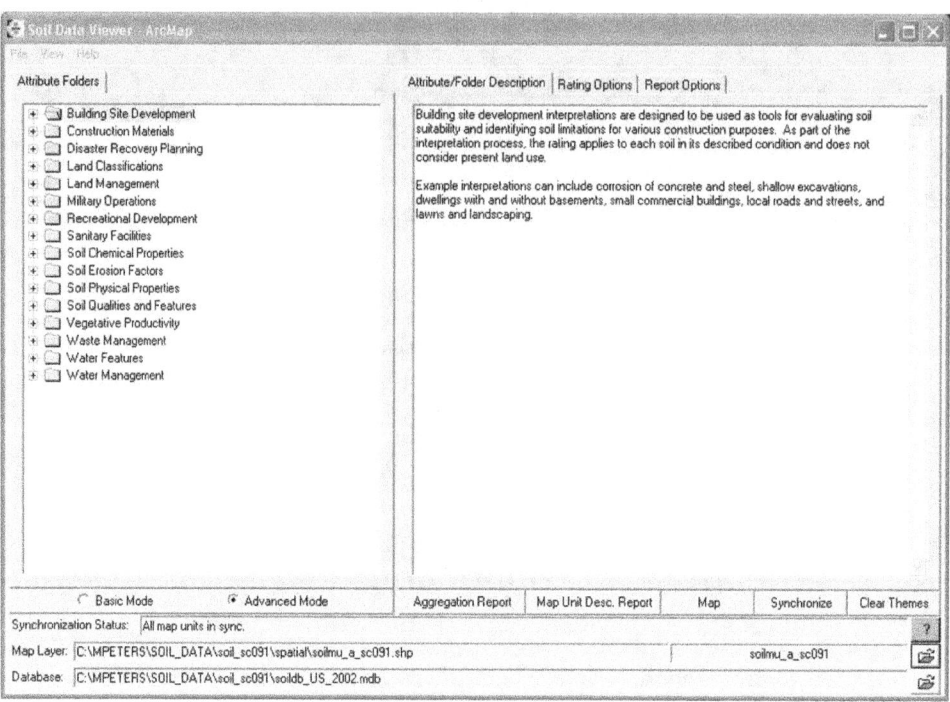

Figure 4.—Soil Data Viewer application window. The attribute description for the selected folder, Building Site Development, is provided on the right.

Similar to the stand-alone version, the ArcGIS extension contains soil attributes organized into folders (fig. 4). Selecting the "Advanced Mode" provides access to more attributes that can be mapped or included in a report. This option is needed to map all of the variables discussed in appendix 1. To produce a SSURGO coverage similar to that of figure 1, expand the Soil Physical Properties folder and select Percent Clay (fig. 5). With the Attribute/Folder Description tab selected (default), clicking on any attribute in the Attribute Folders panel will retrieve the metadata for the selected attribute. As described in the last few lines of the metadata, many attributes have three values: a low, high, and representative (often the default) value.

To parameterize the methods in which the attribute values will be mapped, select the Rating Options tab (fig. 6). In the panel on the right, you have the option to change some of the settings. The first text box contains the default name for the field within the shapefile's attribute table that will contain the value of the soil record. Because changing the names for many counties would have added to the preparation time, the defaults for all eight variables derived from the SDV were accepted.

The next option is the aggregation method. Descriptions of the different methods are provided and each is specific to the selected method of aggregation. The "All Components" method with a tie-break rule of higher values was chosen because our final resolution is 4 km; thus for each map unit the maximum potential value was taken into account.

The final option is related to the depth of the soil component. The "All Layers" option was selected because we could ensure that the entire depth of the component was used over multiple counties.

Now that the parameters are set, the attribute values for the soil property can be exported to ArcMap by clicking on the Map button. After a few seconds, a classified shapefile will appear

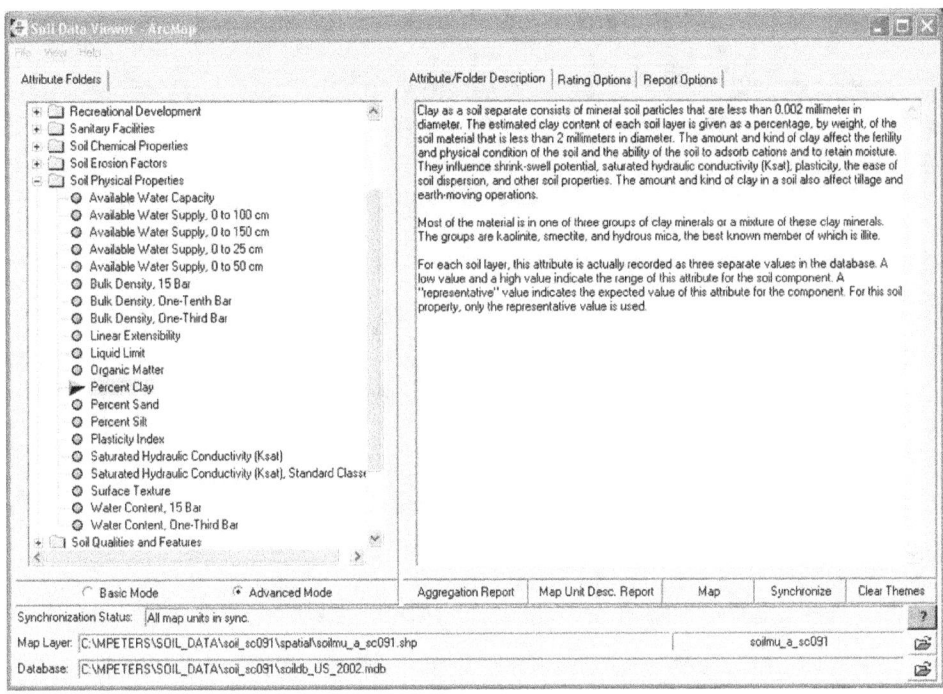

Figure 5.—Soil Data Viewer with the soil physical properties folder expanded and "Percent Clay" selected.

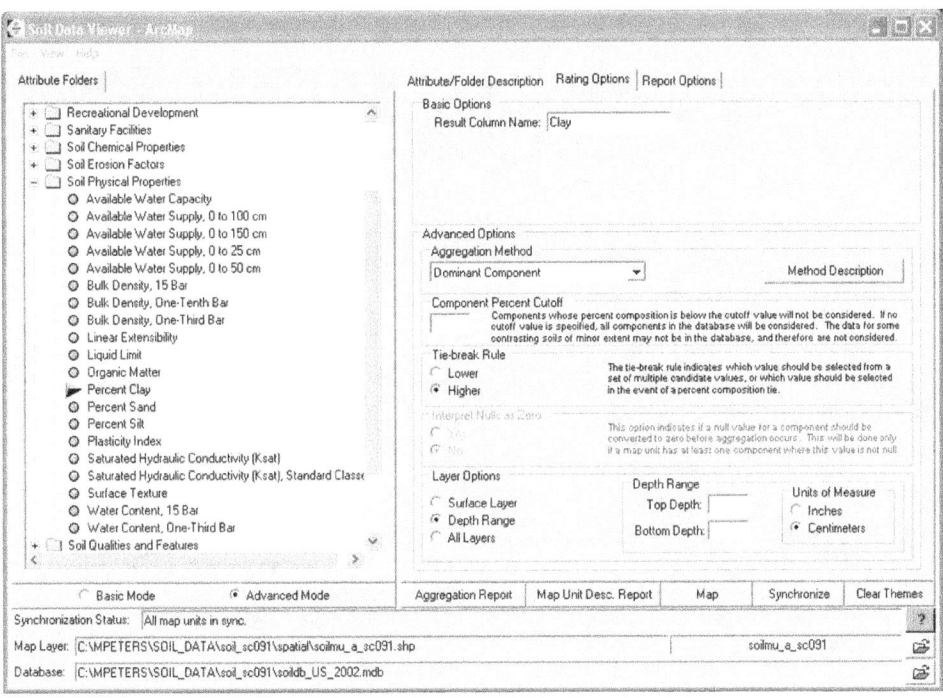

Figure 6.—Soil Data Viewer displaying options for mapping the values of percent clay.

in the ArcMap data frame. This is a temporary file stored in the user's local directory. To permanently save this file, right-click on the layer, move down to the "Data" option, and select "Export Data…," which will allow you to save a copy and rename the shapefile to something meaningful (e.g., oh001_clay.shp). Once the SDV is closed, all temporary shapefiles will be removed from the local directory. This may be a good place to clean up if the system is running low on disk space and you don't want to exit ArcMap or the SDV.

Exporting Custom Soil Data

Although the SDV contains many of the important queries needed to map most of the attributes, there may be attribute values that are not offered within the SDV interface but that are present in the SSURGO database. For example, Iverson et al. (2008) use soil passing sieve numbers 10 and 200 as surrogates for soil texture. Unfortunately, mapping these two attributes is not an option within the SDV. Therefore it may be necessary to export custom queries from the soil database and join them to the map units shapefile. Note that experienced users of R could write a script that reads in the tabular data files and aggregate values for soil horizons and soil components, and to each map unit. Such a script could improve computational times but requires a working knowledge of writing R commands and working with soil data files. Therefore, we will not further pursue this topic.

Custom queries from the SSURGO databases were exported using MS Access 2000, 2003, and 2007. Version 2000 had the capability to directly export a table to DBF format, which is ideal for joining tabular data to a shapefile. This feature, though still present in versions 2003 and 2007, had a 13-character limit on the naming scheme for the exported file. Because the methods are fairly straightforward for the earlier versions of MS Access, the following methods will describe the process under version 2007. It is worth noting that ArcGIS 9.3 and above have the ability to join data from XLS and XLSX formats to shapefiles; however, the sheet containing the records must be identified and this method is rather cumbersome for multiple files.

Three custom queries were created for the newest effort to incorporate fine-scale soil data into our DISTRIB II model framework as follows: information on soil forest productivity (FPROD), soils passing sieve numbers 10 and 200 (NO10 and NO200), and the taxonomic name of soil orders (TAX). Each query contained the fields of "musym" and "mukey" from the mapunit table to provide the symbols for all soil components within the map units. Additionally the fields of "fprod_r" and "cokey" from the coforprod table were included for the FPROD query; "sieveno10_r," "sieveno200_r," and "cokey" from the chorizon table were included for the sieve query; and "taxclname," "taxorder," "taxsuborder," "taxpartsize," and "cokey" from the component table were included in the TAX query. Once these queries are created, they can be copied to other county databases and renamed (ST000_mapunit_qname), where "qname" corresponds to one of the three queries.

After the queries were generated, the records were exported to a CSV file. This format is supported by ArcGIS and can be joined to a shapefile, but further preparation is needed for the taxonomic values. For consistency these files were converted to DBF format. The taxonomic values are stored as strings containing letters which do not map well as a raster grid. To avoid problems and reduce the number of geoprocesses, a numeric value (TAXCODE) was assigned to each taxonomic order (table 2). This step and conversion to DBF format were performed using

Table 2.—Taxonomic soil orders of the eastern United States and a corresponding numeric value

Taxonomic order	TAXCODE
Alfisols	1
Aridisols	2
Entisols	3
Histosols	4
Inceptisols	5
Mollisols	6
Spodosols	7
Ultisols	8
Vertisols	9

R statistical software (R Development Core Team 2010) version 2.12.0 (appendix 6). R's ability to run scripts allowed the final data preparation to be run after all counties within a state were processed. Once complete, the DBF files can be geoprocessed with a Python and AML script.

Geoprocessing Scripts

Python scripts were used to automate the geoprocessing needed to join the exported attribute tables (unless derived from the SDV), dissolve duplicate soil variable values, and convert the shapefile to a raster grid. ArcGIS Model Builder is a quick and convenient way to develop a script, as options are available to export the model to one of three programming languages. We offer our source code in appendix 4 for the various Python scripts used to process our soil variables. Additionally, these scripts are included in the CD-ROM accompanying this General Technical Report. Should a user have access to only ArcGIS and not ArcInfo Workstation, the processing times for many counties can take many days.

After the soil database was prepared and the custom attribute files exported, a script (soil join to raster, see appendix 5) was used to join the queried tables to the soil map units shapefile. This script processes all files in a specified folder, joining the custom attribute tables to the soil shapefile, dissolving records with the same attribute value, and converting the dissolved shapefile to a raster grid (fig. 7). Once the shapefiles of attributes were created from the SDV, another Python script (soil to raster, appendix 4) could be run to convert these files to a grid file. This script is similar to the one previously described in that it processes all files in a specified folder, dissolving records with the same attribute value, and then converting the dissolved shapefile to a raster grid (fig. 8).

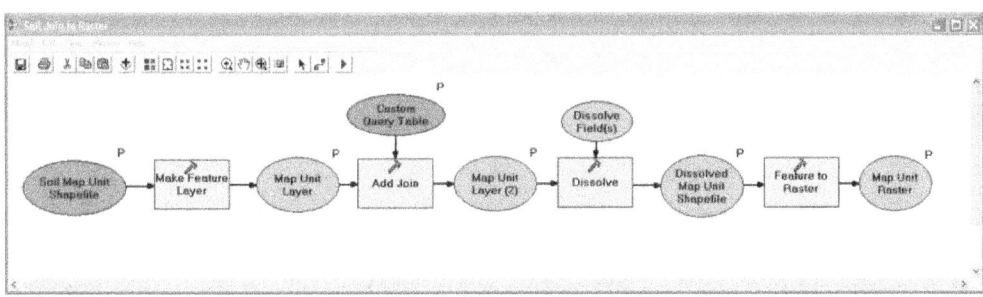

Figure 7.—Schematic of geoprocessing tools to generate raster grids from soil shapefiles with joined custom queries.

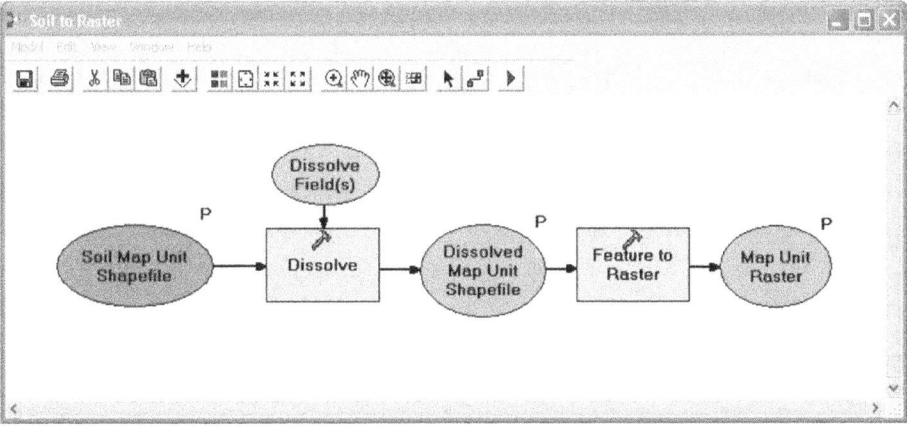

Figure 8.—Schematic of geoprocessing tools to generate raster grids from soil shapefiles.

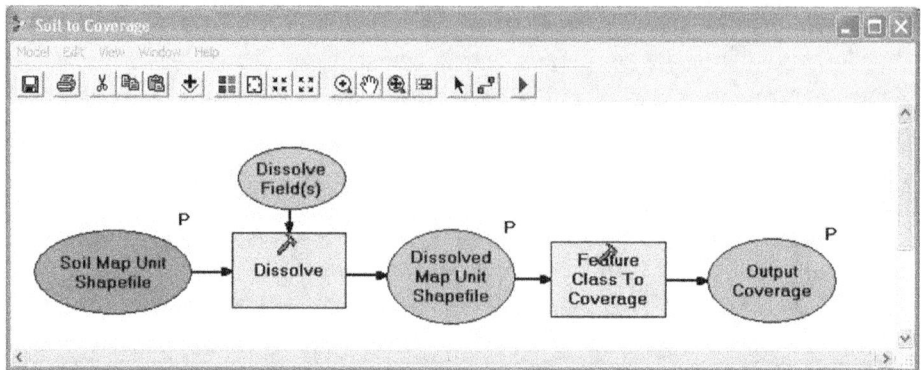

Figure 9.—Schematic of geoprocessing tools to generate an ArcInfo coverage from soil shapefiles with joined custom queries.

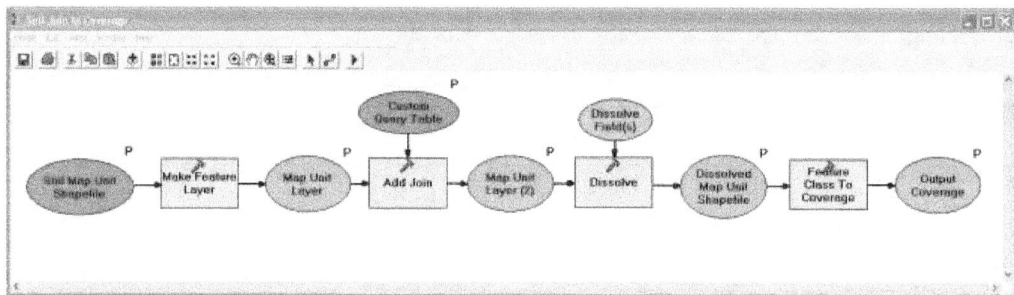

Figure 10.—Schematic of geoprocessing tools to generate an ArcInfo coverage from soil shapefiles.

As previously mentioned, the Python scripts took several days to process all counties in a state. To reduce processing times, parts of the Python scripts were converted to an AML[3] script. Prior to running the AML scripts, a Python script (generate county list) is used to create a text file containing the county codes (ST000). This script processes all shapefiles within a specified folder and extracts the county code from the file name, writing it to a file. The text file is then used to iterate the AML because each state contains a different number of county files.

The AML script was developed from portions of the Python scripts where the conversion from coverage to raster is faster than the geoprocessor. However, a Python script (soil join to raster or soil to raster, appendix 4) was still used to join the exported attribute tables (unless derived from the SDV) and dissolve duplicate soil variable values. Instead of converting the shapefile to a raster file, a conversion to an ArcInfo coverage was needed (figs. 9 and 10).

It is important to understand that the join function in ArcGIS takes the first record when duplicate records are present. Thus, unlike with the SDV, which uses a user-defined aggregation method to summarize unique values for duplicate records, some sort of aggregation will need to be considered. This step should likely be done before running any of the scripts we provide, but could be implemented by altering the code to perform an aggregation. The "Summary Statistics Tool" within the "Analysis Toolbox" can be used to implement a simple aggregation by calculating the minimum, maximum, mean, or standard deviation value for all duplicate map unit symbols within a map unit.

---

[3]We ran AMLs with ArcInfo Workstation 9.3. According to ESRI's Web site, with the release of ArcGIS 10.1, Workstation will no longer be developed. For those who require the application, ESRI recommends using ArcInfo Workstation 10.0 with newer releases (ESRI 2012).

Creating Multiple County/State Coverages

After the Python and AML scripts have been run, the derived output is a county raster grid with 30-m resolution. If the analysis spans multiple counties or even states, it would be advisable to generate a single file containing the attribute values for the study region. Our species distribution model has been run for the eastern United States (east of the 100th meridian); thus to manage the data, all counties within a state were mosaicked to a new raster grid with a 30-m resolution. Upon completion, the individual county shapefiles and grids were compressed for long-term storage. Once the 37 state grids were created, a single eastern U.S. grid was generated by mosaicking (appendix 2: figs. 12 through 22).

A tool is provided within ArcGIS for such a task; however, processing 37 grid files took a considerable amount of time: ~14 days on a personal computer with Core™ 2 Quad processor (Intel®, Santa Clara, CA) and 4 gigabytes of RAM. An alternative to processing all of the states at once involved mosaicking a few neighboring states to a new file and then using the "Mosaic" tool (which adds to an existing file) to allow the process to be broken up. This approach didn't reduce the computational time, but it does allow for minor interruptions (e.g., software updates, restarts, and removal of temporary files). Because each state could have a unique projection (default when obtained from Soil Data Mart), the final projection, a custom Albers 1866 centered over Ohio, was set when the "Mosaic to New Raster" tool was run.

Post-processing

At the time we obtained SSURGO data, the national data set was nearing completion by NRCS; consequently, some counties either had not yet been mapped, contained only tabular data, or had other missing information. Even when the final data set is complete, there may still be locations where information is missing, such as large bodies of water or public lands that were not surveyed (NRCS 2011a). Conditions within the landscape prevent NRCS staff from mapping some areas. To avoid modeling with "No Data" because the final SSURGO product hadn't been released or because data will not be collected, more generalized STATSGO data were used to fill these gaps. A GIS model (fig. 11) was developed to examine each 30-m cell, and where values of "No Data" were present in the SSURGO grid, cell values were replaced with STATSGO values.

Post-process Soil Variable

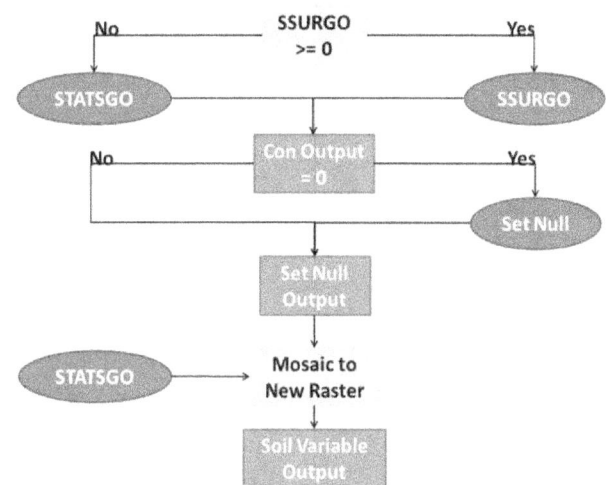

Figure 11.—Schematic of geoprocessing used to fill gaps within SSURGO with STATSGO values, and then create a new raster file for the completed soil variable.

The model uses a conditional statement (SSURGO >= 0, SSURGO, STATSGO) to test against SSURGO values and where values are returned as false, STATSGO values are used.

At this point the coverage still contains values of "No Data." The "Set Null" tool was used to remove values from the conditional output equal to zero. Once the zeros are changed to "No Data," the null output and STATSGO coverage are mosaicked into a new raster grid, where the SSURGO values from the null output are used first, followed by the STATSGO values. This

Table 3.—Select zonal statistics of 11 soil attributes at 4-km resolution for SSURGO and STATSGO soil data for the eastern United States

	SSURGO				STATSGO			
	Min	Mean	Max	SD	Min	Mean	Max	SD
Available water supply (cm)	0.1	21.65	77.69	7.0	1.11	21.34	77.69	7.2
Bulk density	0.15	1.47	2.18	0.14	0.15	1.31	1.95	0.34
Percent clay	0.2	27.51	85	12.56	0.5	20.32	80.9	13.18
Forest productivity (ft^3/acre/year)	2	81.46	211	28.73	14	90.0	200	43.8
K factor	0.02	0.36	10.95	0.12	0.02	0.27	0.64	0.12
Organic matter (%)	0.01	3.81	140.78	8.25	0.05	2.57	89.5	7.21
Permeability (cm/hr)	1	29.56	705	34.84	0.03	19.35	141.14	24.1
pH	2.1	6.28	9.3	1.03	3.6	5.53	8.7	1.72
Rock depth (cm)	2	150.98	251	40.52	4	150.15	217	54.63
Sieve 10 (%)	2	88.83	100	11.83	38.35	88.27	100	11.98
Sieve 200 (%)	1	59.97	100	24.65	3.58	60.11	97.5	21.51

post-processing creates a complete grid that contains "No Data" values only if the SSURGO and STATSGO data were null. Depending on the soil variable, the conditional statement can be changed to account for values that should be greater than zero.[4] Now that the entire eastern United States had been processed at a fine resolution with minimal gaps, aggregation can be performed to generate the 4-km data set to use in our SDM, among other purposes.

The completed grids with a 30-m resolution over the entire eastern United States are very large (~35-45 gigabytes). The massive file size is a result of the file format, 32-bit floating point for most variables. Most of the attributes contain decimal values with a small range of variation, so it is important to distinguish changes among map units. One way that we reduced the file sizes (~50%) was to multiply the grids by 10 or 100 and convert the floating points to 16-bit signed integers. This process could have been performed before the conversion to a raster file by adding a new field to the shapefiles. However, it was unforeseen that the final files would be so large.

Summary Statistics

For the eastern U.S. 4-km soil coverages, statistics were calculated for both SSURGO and STATSGO values (table 3). Zonal statistics were calculated in an iterative manner for 56 groups containing ~10,000 of the 4-km polygon grids because a memory limit within the software resulted in the reporting of values at the center of the 4-km grid. This process produced 56 output files containing all of the statistics calculated from the "Zonal Statistics to Table" tool. Joining 56 files to the 4-km polygon grid shapefile is not efficient. Therefore R commands were used to read in all DBF files and write the data to a single file (appendix 6). Summaries for the entire eastern United States and the 37 states were compiled for each variable from SSURGO and STATSGO data to identify any benefits gained from the fine-scale data (table 1). The 4-km zonal statistics summaries are included on the accompanying CD-ROM.

---

[4]Variables such as bulk density and K-factor range from near zero to 0.1 and greater; thus a conditional statement of ≥0 would be inappropriate because it would keep false values. Likewise, pH values of 0 may be erroneous, in which case it may be better to use values from STATSGO.

RESULTS

Fine-scale soil data (SSURGO) were prepared for the eastern United States for use in a species distribution model (SDM). Twelve soil attributes (table 1) mapped at 30-m grids were statistically summarized at a 4-km resolution to create a more manageable data set in general and to generate a scale-compatible data set for our SDM framework. Calculating zonal statistics and tabulating the area of occupancy were the methods used to summarize the data as they provide a more accurate value over other methods of aggregation. State summaries based on the 30-m values were also calculated and are presented in appendix 3.

Comparing the minimum, maximum, and mean SSURGO values for the eastern United States to STATSGO values reveals that the minimum and maximum values are often outside the range of STATSGO values (table 3). The mean values of SSURGO are also greater than STATSGO, with the exception of forest productivity and percentage of soil passing sieve number 200. Differences between the two data sets are most likely due to how SSURGO is aggregated into STATSGO, which seems to underestimate many of the 11 soil properties our SDM considers.

DISCUSSION

Our methodology appears to follow that of NRCS' parallel effort, which we did not know about. The Natural Resources Conservation Service developed a gridded 10-m version of SSURGO data for the contiguous United States. This "snapshot" data set is composed of a 10-m grid of integer values representing the soil map unit's "mukey" and a geodatabase containing the soil attribute tables (Sharon Waltman, NRCS, pers. communication, January 2011). Joining attribute data to a single grid has benefits, in that the grid locations are consistent in any output coverage. Output data from our method do not have consistent grid locations because the attribute values used in the conversion to grids were dissolved. We suspect that by creating a single grid from map units and joining attribute data to them, slight differences will be present between the snapshot data and our coverages. However, each methodology has benefits and limitations.

For large (state and multi-state) areas, researchers in need of many soil properties might find the snapshot data set a more efficient resource because much of the processing has been performed. As the term "snapshot" implies, however, this data set is time sensitive and might not include the latest data values. Additionally, depending on the application, the single grid can result in aggregation errors, where grid cells on the border of two or more map units will most likely report the dominant map unit.

For areas large or small, researchers needing a small number of soil attributes might use the methods outlined in this report to generate their own data coverages. Advantages include processing an area of interest, utilizing custom queries to produce unique attributes, and the ability to control the aggregation methods. However, like the snapshot, output coverages will be time sensitive.

While obtaining soil data, generating attribute coverages, and producing a continuous grid, we had to resolve several major issues. These issues dealt with time constraints, processing non-numeric values, missing values, and storage space and backup of the data.

Obtaining fine-scale variables over the large extent of our project was by no means a quick job. Counties had to be processed and compiled to state coverages, which were then used to generate a single coverage for the eastern United States. This process then had to be carried out for 12 variables, requiring a lot of user interaction. Using scripts to automate many of the geoprocessing tasks on individual files helped reduce much of the interaction needed to set up and run processes on each file. This batch mode approach allowed the data processing to be performed overnight and during weekends or while other files were prepared.

Even though the scripts automated much of the work, the ArcGIS geoprocessor took several hours to run certain processes, during which time counties for another state could be prepared. We were still productive during the downtime of a running script, but we felt that the runtime was too long. The runtime of the Python scripts was improved by converting a portion of the scripts to AML; consequently days became hours. Despite this major accomplishment, each of eight variables still had to be generated from the SDV, which on average took about 24 staff hours. This amount of time seemed more reasonable as we could begin to mosaic counties into a state coverage while preparing the data files for the next state.

Early in the processing, we discovered a problem related to values stored as strings. Of the 12 variables that we were processing, 2 were non-numeric, or contained string values: the taxonomic orders and decimal values of Kffact. Because the SDV exported Kffact values without a leading zero (e.g., .53), ArcMap treats them as strings rather than as floating points. Therefore these two variables had to be converted to an integer (taxonomic) and a floating point (Kffact) value. Taxonomic names were matched to an integer value by using R statistical software as we wanted to convert the custom query from a CSV to a DBF file format. Kffact was already a shapefile produced by the SDV and we simply added a new field to the attribute table via the script used to process it.

Another issue related to the attribute shapefiles produced by the SDV involves values representing water. Map units that delineate water bodies contain null values when attributes are exported from the SDV. Permanently saving the temporary shapefiles by exporting to a new shapefile converts null values to zero, which can be problematic. Because we knew that gaps within the SSURGO data set would be filled with values from STATSGO, we didn't worry about areas of water containing zeros. These artificial zeros could be removed and converted back to null values during the post-processing, where zeros would be reported if STATSGO contained zeros.

Storage of all the files we had obtained from NRCS and generated via the processing quickly began to fill up our storage space (500-gigabyte hard drive). Therefore once a state was completed, all files were compressed for storage and the originals were deleted to free up disk space. Shapefiles derived from the SDV, the final raster grids, and the DBF tables from the custom queries for each county were saved during this project. These steps ensured that the preliminary files were retained if we need to start from the beginning. Additionally, backing up these files was a challenge because dual-layer DVDs held an insufficient amount of data and Blu-ray DVDs were expensive. Our solution was to split the files among several hard drives to ensure redundancy should one fail.

Although the methods described to develop a multi-regional fine-scale coverage of soil data produced a continuous data set, some caveats should be considered when using these data. Our final SSURGO coverage contained gaps caused by missing data. The gaps reflect areas that, at the time of download, contained only tabular data, were public lands where a survey was not conducted, or included a large body of water. These gaps, if unfilled, are unacceptable for modeling species distributions because they would falsely classify suitable habitat, introducing a greater amount of error into the model output. To remove these gaps and provide real values, STATSGO soil data were used to perform a multistep conditional statement that produced a continuous grid of values.

Certainly a major benefit of using SSURGO over STATSGO soil data is the improved delineation of map units. A less generalized coverage lends itself to a more accurate habitat model by permitting a finer resolution to be used for the output. The availability of both soil data sets as vector coverages means that fine-scale grids (30 m) can be generated and resampled or statistically summarized to a coarser resolution with averages calculated at a greater accuracy than if only coarse-scale data were used.

CONCLUSIONS

The procedures described in this report are specific to the needs of our modeling efforts, where fine-scale soil data over a large extent were sought to improve the prediction accuracy and reliability of our species distribution model. As with many computational processes, there are other ways in which the results presented here could have been derived and we acknowledge that our method may not be appropriate for every situation. However, we offer a framework which others can use as a starting point to develop and process fine-scale soil data.

The overall methodology development and processing took months to produce the fine-scale results presented in appendix 2: figures 12-22, mainly due to the long computational time of the initial Python scripts and time spent obtaining the individual county files. The efficiency of the scripts was improved by splitting the processes among Python and AML scripts. Even with the improved scripts, the process could be streamlined by (1) having multiple technicians obtain, prepare, and process the data; (2) using several high-performance computers to process the mosaicking of multiple counties; and (3) testing the methods to ensure the accuracy of the output. Much of the time early in the processing was devoted to obtaining the data and formulating the methodology to create a single fine-scale coverage which could be resampled to coarser resolutions.

Our previous research indicates that the 12 soil attributes presented here are important predictors of habitats for many tree species in the eastern United States (Iverson et al. 2008) and for many insects in Europe (Titeux et al. 2009). Researchers in a variety of fields (e.g., ecology, geology, hydrology) could benefit from including fine-scale soil data in their models; accordingly, we offer our statistically resampled data at a 4-km resolution. To limit the file sizes we provide a 4-km polygon grid and tabular summaries for each of the 12 soil variables. Users can then generate individual shapefiles or raster grids based on the statistical summary data.

ACKNOWLEDGMENTS

We are grateful to the many people who have collected, have prepared, and maintain the digital county soil survey (SSURGO) and state soil survey (STATSGO) data available online from the USDA Natural Resources Conservation Service. We also thank the reviewers who improved this report.

LITERATURE CITED

ESRI. 2012. **Deprecation plan for ArcGIS 10.0 and ArcGIS 10.2.** Last updated June 7, 2012. Available at http://downloads2.esri.com/support/TechArticles/ ArcGIS10and101Deprecation_Plan.pdf. (Accessed May 31, 2013).

Iverson, L.R.; Prasad, A.M.; Hale, B.J.; Sutherland, E.K. 1999. **Atlas of current and potential future distributions of common trees of the eastern United States.** Gen. Tech. Rep. NE-265. Radnor, PA: U.S. Department of Agriculture, Forest Service, Northeastern Research Station. 245 p.

Iverson, L.R.; Prasad, A.M.; Matthews, S.N.; Peters, M. 2008. **Estimating potential habitat for 134 eastern US tree species under six climate scenarios.** Forest Ecology and Management. 254: 390-406.

Iverson, L.R.; Prasad, A.M.; Matthews, S.N.; Peters, M.P. 2011. **Lessons learned while integrating habitat, dispersal, disturbance, and life-history traits into species habitat models under climate change.** Ecosystems. 14: 1005-1020.

Matthews, S.N.; Iverson, L.R.; Prasad, A.M.; Peters, M.P.; Rodewald, P.G. 2011. **Modifying climate change habitat models using tree species-specific assessments of model uncertainty and life history-factors.** Forest Ecology and Management. 262: 1460-1472.

Natural Resources Conservation Service (NRCS). 2008. **Soil Data Viewer 5.2.** Available at http://soils.usda.gov/sdv/download.html. (Accessed May 31, 2013).

Natural Resources Conservation Service (NRCS). 2009. **Soil Survey Geographic (SSURGO) database for counties of Alabama, Arkansas, Connecticut, Delaware, District of Columbia, Florida, Georgia, Illinois, Indiana, Iowa, Kansas, Kentucky, Louisiana, Maine, Maryland, Massachusetts, Michigan, Minnesota, Mississippi, Missouri, Nebraska, New Hampshire, New Jersey, New York, North Carolina, North Dakota, Ohio, Oklahoma, Pennsylvania, Rhode Island, South Carolina, South Dakota, Tennessee, Texas, Vermont, Virginia, West Virginia, Wisconsin.** Available at http:// soildatamart.nrcs.usda.gov/State.aspx. (Accessed between August 2009 and November 2010).

Natural Resources Conservation Service (NRCS). 2011a. **Determining soil data availability.** Available at http://soildatamart.nrcs.usda.gov/documents/DeterminingSoilDataAvailability. pdf. (Accessed July 27, 2011).

Natural Resources Conservation Service (NRCS). 2011b. **Soil Survey Program.** 2011. http://www.nrcs.usda.gov/wps/portal/nrcs/main/ms/soils/surveys/. (Accessed May 25, 2011).

Prasad, A.M.; Iverson, L.R.; Liaw, A. 2006. **Newer classification and regression tree techniques: Bagging and Random Forests for ecological prediction.** Ecosystems. 9: 181-199.

Prasad, A.M.; Iverson, L.R.; Matthews, S.; Peters, M. 2007-ongoing. **A climate change atlas for 134 forest tree species of the eastern United States [Database].** Available at http://www.nrs.fs.fed.us/atlas/tree. (Accessed May 31, 2013).

R Development Core Team. 2010. **R: a language and environment for statistical computing.** Vienna, Austria: R Foundation for Statistical Computing. Available at http://www.R-project.org/. (Accessed June 7, 2013).

Titeux, N.; Maes, D.; Marmion, M.; Luoto, M.; Heikkinen, R.K. 2009. **Inclusion of soil data improves the performance of bioclimatic envelope models for insect species distributions in temperate Europe.** Journal of Biogeography. 36: 1459-1473.

APPENDIX 1: DESCRIPTIONS OF SOIL VARIABLES

The following information, with the exception of the taxonomic orders, was extracted from the Soil Data Viewer (Natural Resources Conservation Service [NRCS] 2008) or the metadata for the soil database tables (NRCS 2009).

Available Water Supply (cm, to 150 cm)

Available water supply (AWS) is the total volume of water (in centimeters) that should be available to plants when the soil, inclusive of rock fragments, is at field capacity. It is commonly estimated as the amount of water held between field capacity and the wilting point, with corrections for salinity, rock fragments, and rooting depth. AWS is reported as a single value (in centimeters) of water for the specified depth of the soil. AWS is calculated as the available water capacity times the thickness of each soil horizon to a specified depth.

For each soil layer, available water capacity, used in the computation of AWS, is recorded as three separate values in the database. A low value and a high value indicate the range of this attribute for the soil component. A "representative" value indicates the expected value of this attribute for the component. For the derivation of AWS, only the representative value for available water capacity is used.

The available water supply for each map unit component is computed as described above and then aggregated to a single value for the map unit by the process described below.

A map unit typically consists of one or more "components." A component is either some type of soil or some nonsoil entity, e.g., rock outcrop. For the attribute being aggregated (e.g., available water supply), the first step of the aggregation process is to derive one attribute value for each of a map unit's components. From this set of component attributes, the next step of the process is to derive a single value that represents the map unit as a whole. Once a single value for each map unit is derived, a thematic map for the map units can be generated. Aggregation is needed because map units rather than components are delineated on the soil maps.

The composition of each component in a map unit is recorded as a percentage. A composition of 60 indicates that the component typically makes up approximately 60 percent of the map unit.

--(NRCS 2008, 2009)

Soil Bulk Density (g/cm)

Bulk density, one-third bar, is the oven dry weight of the soil material less than 2 mm in size per unit volume of soil at water tension of 1/3 bar, expressed in grams per cubic centimeter. Bulk density data are used to compute linear extensibility, shrink-swell potential, available water capacity, total pore space, and other soil properties. The moist bulk density of a soil indicates the pore space available for water and roots. Depending on soil texture, a bulk density of more than 1.4 can restrict water storage and root penetration. Moist bulk density is influenced by texture, kind of clay, content of organic matter, and soil structure.

For each soil layer, this attribute is actually recorded as three separate values in the database. A low value and a high value indicate the range of this attribute for the soil component. A "representative" value indicates the expected value of this attribute for the component. For this soil property, only the representative value is used.

--(NRCS 2009)

Percent Clay (<0.002 mm)

Clay as a soil separate consists of mineral soil particles that are less than 0.002 millimeter in diameter. The estimated clay content of each soil layer is given as a percentage, by weight, of the soil material that is less than 2 millimeters in diameter. The amount and kind of clay affect the fertility and physical condition of the soil and the ability of the soil to adsorb cations and to retain moisture. They influence shrink-swell potential, saturated hydraulic conductivity (Ksat), plasticity, the ease of soil dispersion, and other soil properties. The amount and kind of clay in a soil also affect tillage and earth-moving operations.

Most of the material is in one of three groups of clay minerals or a mixture of these clay minerals. The groups are kaolinite, smectite, and hydrous mica, the best known member of which is illite.

For each soil layer, this attribute is actually recorded as three separate values in the database. A low value and a high value indicate the range of this attribute for the soil component. A "representative" value indicates the expected value of this attribute for the component. For this soil property, only the representative value is used.

--(NRCS 2008, 2009)

Potential Soil Productivity (ft^3/acre/year)

This variable is an estimate of the capability of the soil to support the annual growth of forest overstory tree species. Forest productivity is the volume of wood fiber that is the yield likely to be produced by the most important tree species. This number, expressed as cubic feet per acre per year and calculated at the age of culmination of the mean annual increment (CMAI), indicates the amount of fiber produced in a fully stocked, even-aged, unmanaged stand.

This attribute is actually recorded as three separate values in the database. A low value and a high value indicate the range of this attribute for the soil component. A "representative" value indicates the expected value of this attribute for the component. For this attribute, only the representative value is used.

--(NRCS 2008, 2009)

Soil Erodibility Factor, rock free (K)

Erosion factor K indicates the susceptibility of a soil to sheet and rill erosion by water. K factor is one of six factors used in the Universal Soil Loss Equation (USLE) and the Revised Universal Soil Loss Equation (RUSLE) to predict the average annual rate of soil loss by sheet and rill erosion in tons per acre per year. The estimates are based primarily on percentage of silt, sand, and organic matter and on soil structure and saturated hydraulic conductivity (Ksat). Values of K range from 0.02 to 0.69. Other factors being equal, the higher the value, the more susceptible the soil is to sheet and rill erosion by water.

Erosion factor "Kf (rock free)" indicates the erodibility of the fine-earth fraction, or the material less than 2 millimeters in size.

--(NRCS 2008, 2009)

Organic Matter Content (% by weight)

Organic matter is the plant and animal residue in the soil at various stages of decomposition. The estimated content of organic matter is expressed as a percentage, by weight, of the soil material that is less than 2 mm in diameter.

The content of organic matter in a soil can be maintained by returning crop residue to the soil. Organic matter has a positive effect on available water capacity, water infiltration, soil organism activity, and tilth. It is a source of nitrogen and other nutrients for crops and soil organisms. An irregular distribution of organic carbon with depth may indicate different episodes of soil deposition or soil formation. Soils that are very high in organic matter have poor engineering properties and subside upon drying.

For each soil layer, this attribute is actually recorded as three separate values in the database. A low value and a high value indicate the range of this attribute for the soil component. A "representative" value indicates the expected value of this attribute for the component. For this soil property, only the representative value is used.

--(NRCS 2008, 2009)

Soil Permeability Rate (cm/hr)

Saturated hydraulic conductivity (Ksat) refers to the ease with which pores in a saturated soil transmit water. The estimates are expressed in terms of micrometers per second. They are based on soil characteristics observed in the field, particularly structure, porosity, and texture. Saturated hydraulic conductivity is considered in the design of soil drainage systems and septic tank absorption fields.

For each soil layer, this attribute is actually recorded as three separate values in the database. A low value and a high value indicate the range of this attribute for the soil component. A "representative" value indicates the expected value of this attribute for the component. For this soil property, only the representative value is used.

The numeric Ksat values have been grouped according to standard Ksat class limits. The classes are:

Very low: 0.00 to 0.01
Low: 0.01 to 0.1

Moderately low: 0.1 to 1.0
Moderately high: 1 to 10
High: 10 to 100
Very high: 100 to 705

--(NRCS 2008, 2009)

Soil pH

Soil reaction is a measure of acidity or alkalinity. It is important in selecting crops and other plants, in evaluating soil amendments for fertility and stabilization, and in determining the risk of corrosion. In general, soils that are either highly alkaline or highly acid are likely to be very corrosive to steel. The most common soil laboratory measurement of pH is the 1:1 water method. A crushed soil sample is mixed with an equal amount of water, and a measurement is made of the suspension.

For each soil layer, this attribute is actually recorded as three separate values in the database. A low value and a high value indicate the range of this attribute for the soil component. A "representative" value indicates the expected value of this attribute for the component. For this soil property, only the representative value is used.

--(NRCS 2008, 2009)

Depth to Bedrock (cm)

A "restrictive layer" is a nearly continuous layer that has one or more physical, chemical, or thermal properties that significantly impede the movement of water and air through the soil or that restrict roots or otherwise provide an unfavorable root environment. Examples are bedrock, cemented layers, dense layers, and frozen layers.

This theme presents the depth to any type of restrictive layer that is described for each map unit. If more than one type of restrictive layer is described for an individual soil type, the depth to the shallowest one is presented. If no restrictive layer is described in a map unit, it is represented by the "> 200" depth class.

This attribute is actually recorded as three separate values in the database. A low value and a high value indicate the range of this attribute for the soil component. A "representative" value indicates the expected value of this attribute for the component. For this soil property, only the representative value is used.

--(NRCS 2008, 2009)

Soil Passing Sieve No. 10 (coarse)

Variable is related to the coarse texture of soils, that being the soil fraction passing a number 10 sieve (2.00mm square opening) as a weight percentage of the less than 3 inch (76.4mm) fraction.

--(NRCS 2008, 2009)

Soil Passing Sieve No. 200 (fine)

Variable is related to the coarse texture of soils, that being the soil fraction passing a number 200 sieve (0.074mm square opening) as a weight percentage of the less than 3 inch (76.4mm) fraction.

--(NRCS 2008, 2009)

Taxonomic Orders

Soil map units were identified by taxonomic orders and mapped. Ten values (0-9) represent nine orders (Alfisols, Aridisols, Entisols, Histosols, Inceptisols, Mollisols, Spodosols, Ultisols, Vertisols) and a value of No Data. For ease in analysis, the orders were converted to the numeric values TAXCODE (1, 2, 3, 4, 5, 6, 7, 8, 9), which correspond to the names in alphabetical order.

APPENDIX 2: SOIL VARIABLE MAPS

Fine-scale data for 12 attributes were compiled from SSURGO data and include STATSGO values where gaps exist. The following 11 figures (4-km resolution) were derived from 30-m data sets for the eastern United States by using zonal statistics to calculate the minimum, maximum, mean, range, standard deviation, sum, minority, majority, and median values for each 4-km grid. The mean value for each soil attribute is displayed; however, we include the 4-km grid and zonal statistics tables on the supplementary CD-ROM.

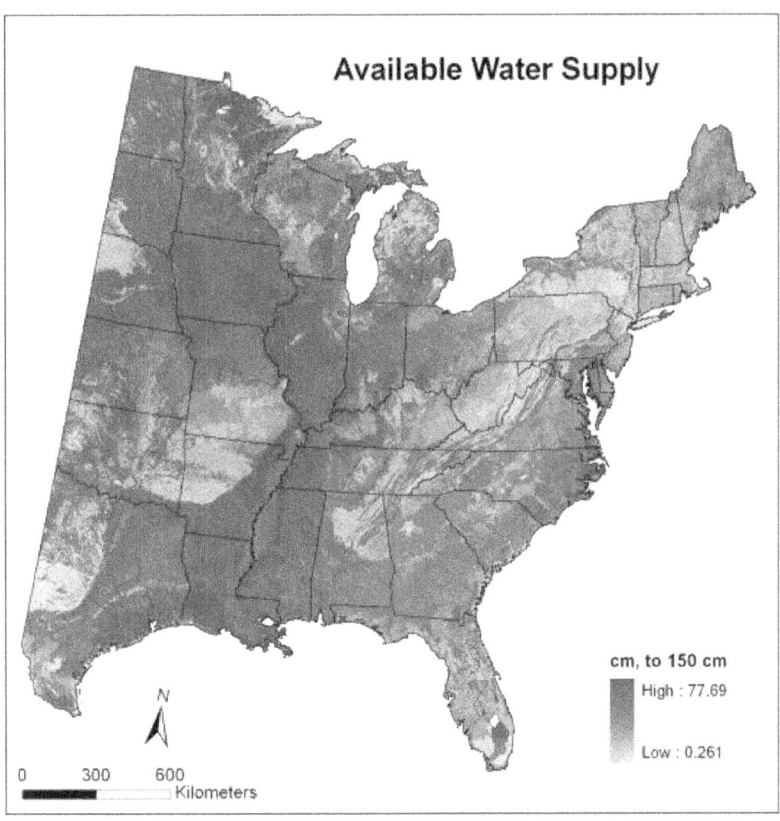

Figure 12.—Mean available water supply in eastern U.S. soils, based on SSURGO data. Number of 4-km grids: 265,091. Mean available water supply: 21.65 cm, to 150 cm.

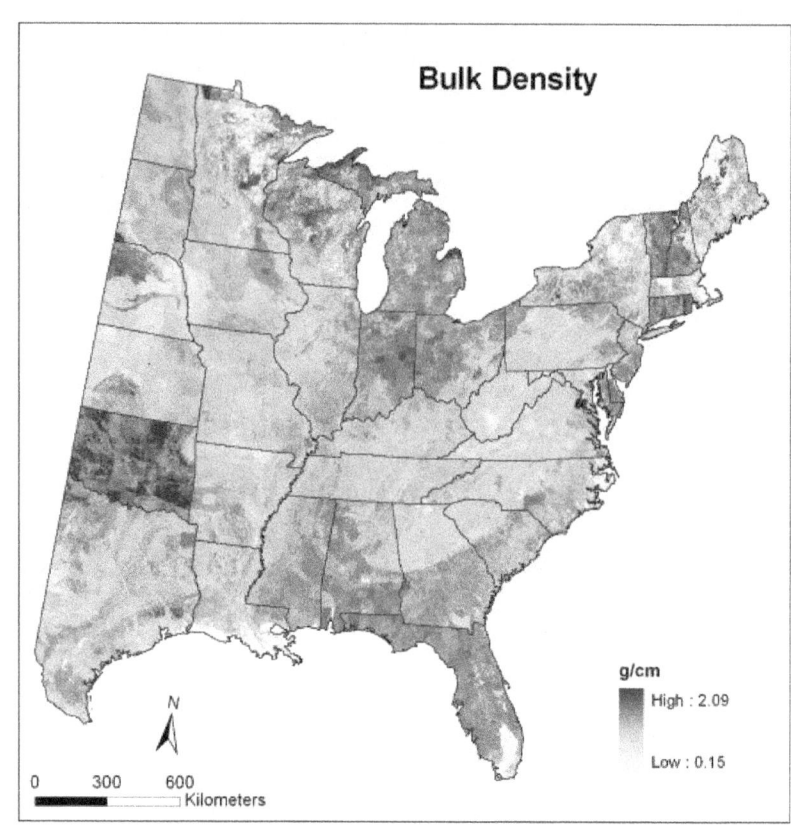

Figure 13.—Mean bulk density values of eastern U.S. soils, based on SSURGO data. Number of 4-km grids: 264,768. Mean bulk density: 1.47 g/cm.

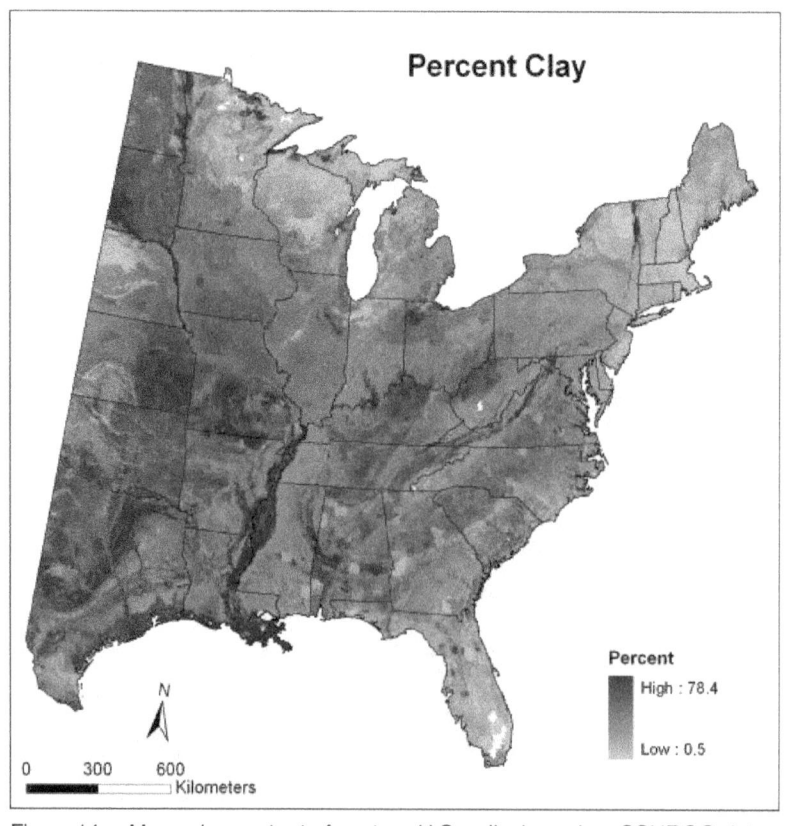

Figure 14.—Mean clay content of eastern U.S. soils, based on SSURGO data. Number of 4-km grids: 264,553. Mean percent clay: 27.5 percent.

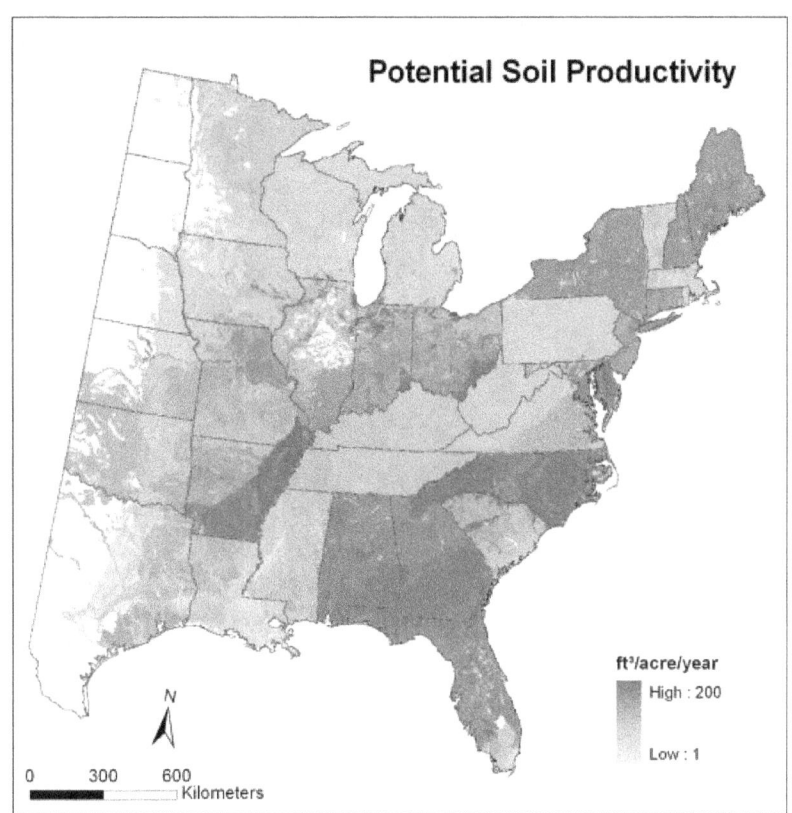

Figure 15.—Mean potential productivity of eastern U.S. soils, based on STATSGO/SSURGO data. Number of 4-km grids: 226,528. Mean soil productivity: 82 ft^3/acre/year. Variation by state is due to variation among dominant tree species or use of STATSGO in filling gaps.

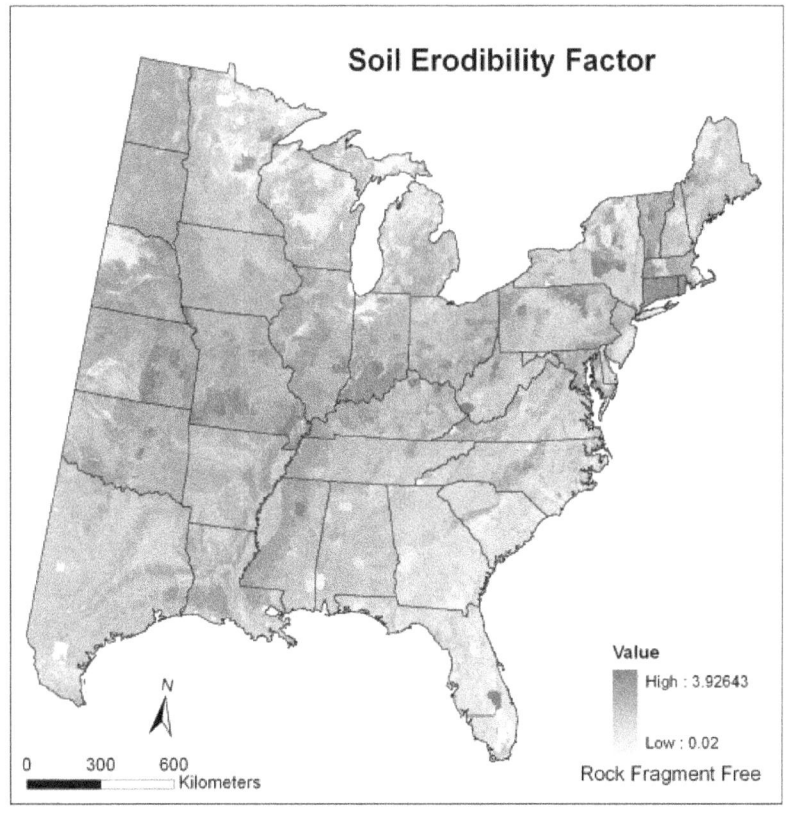

Figure 16.—Mean erodibility factor values of eastern U.S. soils, based on SSURGO data. Number of 4-km grids: 263,845. Mean erodibility factor (K): 0.36.

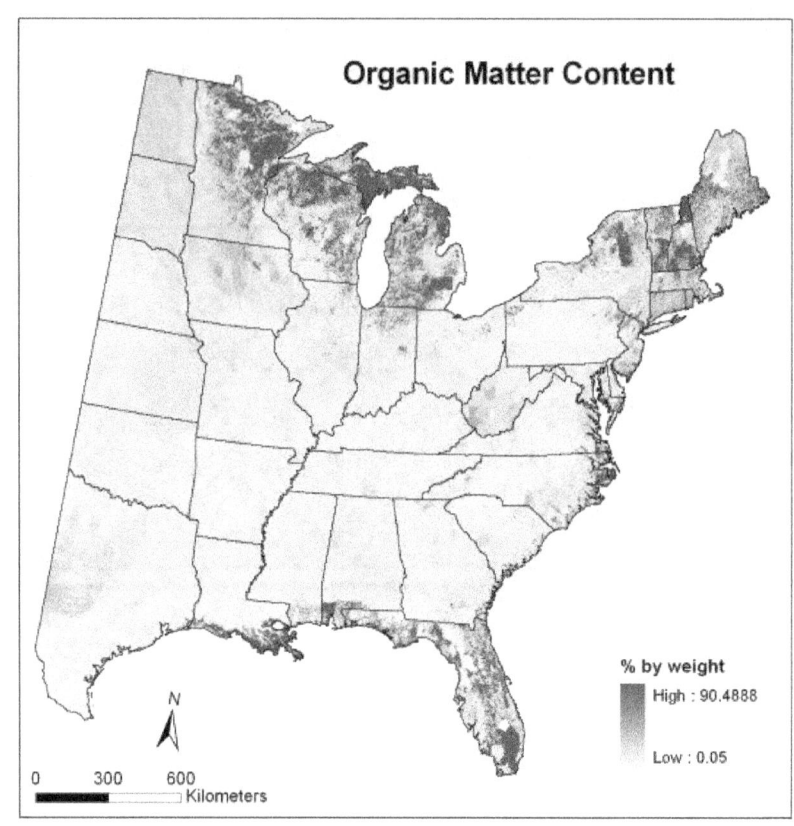

Figure 17.—Mean organic matter content of eastern U.S. soils, based on SSURGO data. Number of 4-km grids: 264,386. Mean organic matter: 3.8 percent by weight.

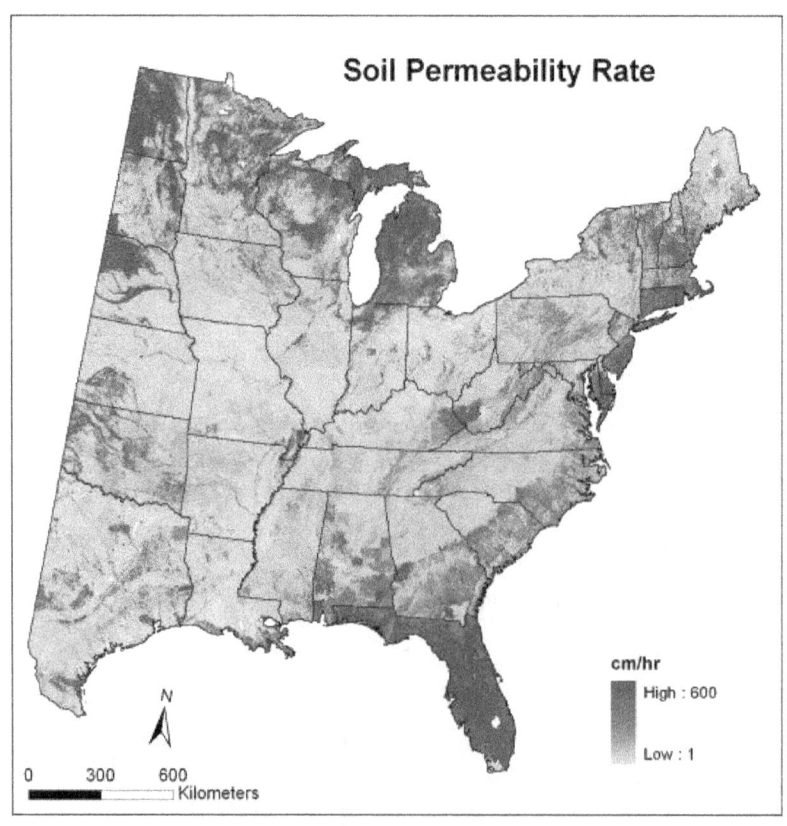

Figure 18.—Mean permeability rates of eastern U.S. soils, based on SSURGO data. Number of 4-km grids: 264,463. Mean permeability rate: 30 cm/hour.

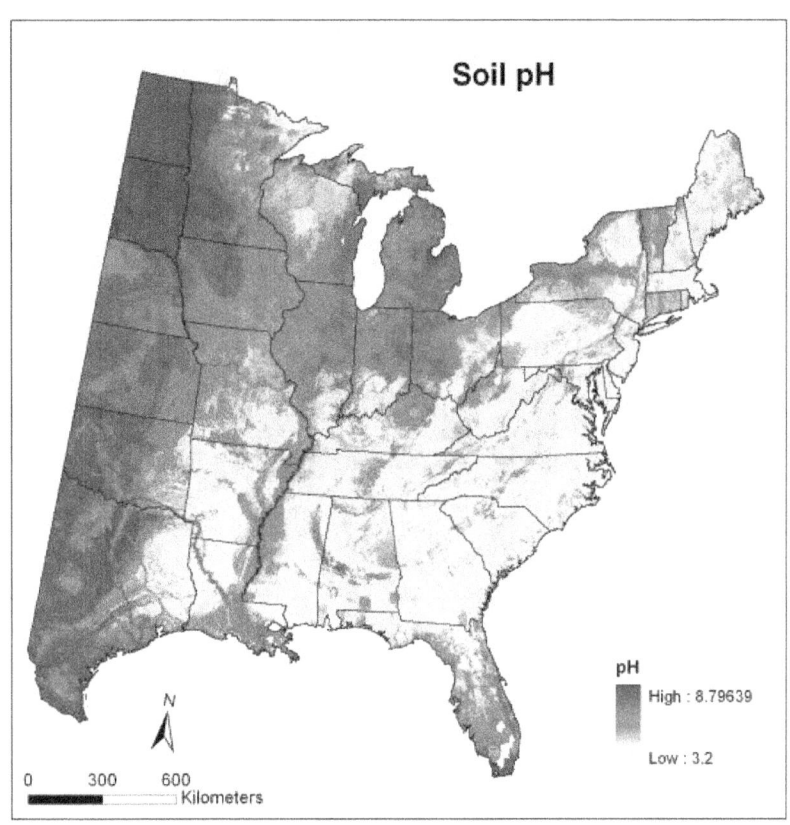

Figure 19.—Mean pH of eastern U.S. soils, based on SSURGO data. Number of 4-km grids: 264,312. Mean pH: 6.3.

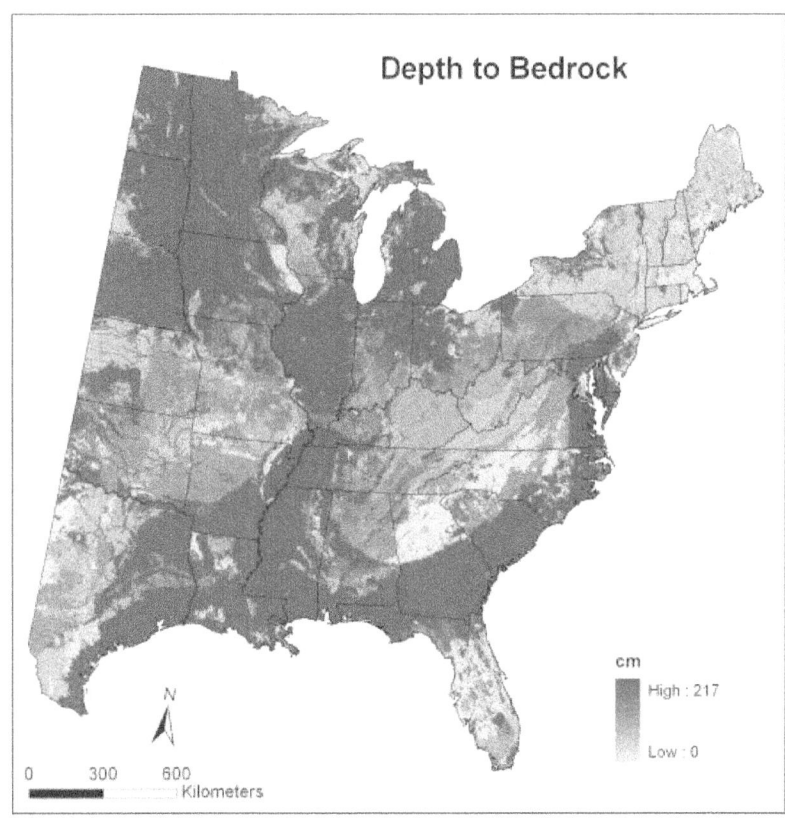

Figure 20.—Mean depth to bedrock in the eastern United States, based on SSURGO data. Number of 4-km grids: 267,745. Mean depth to bedrock: 151 cm.

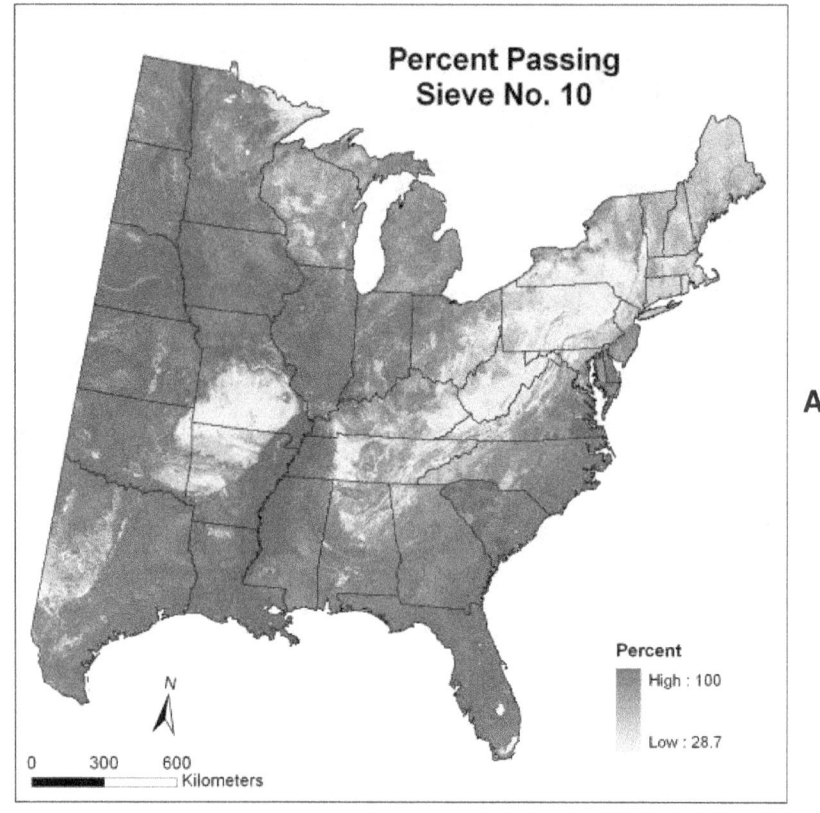

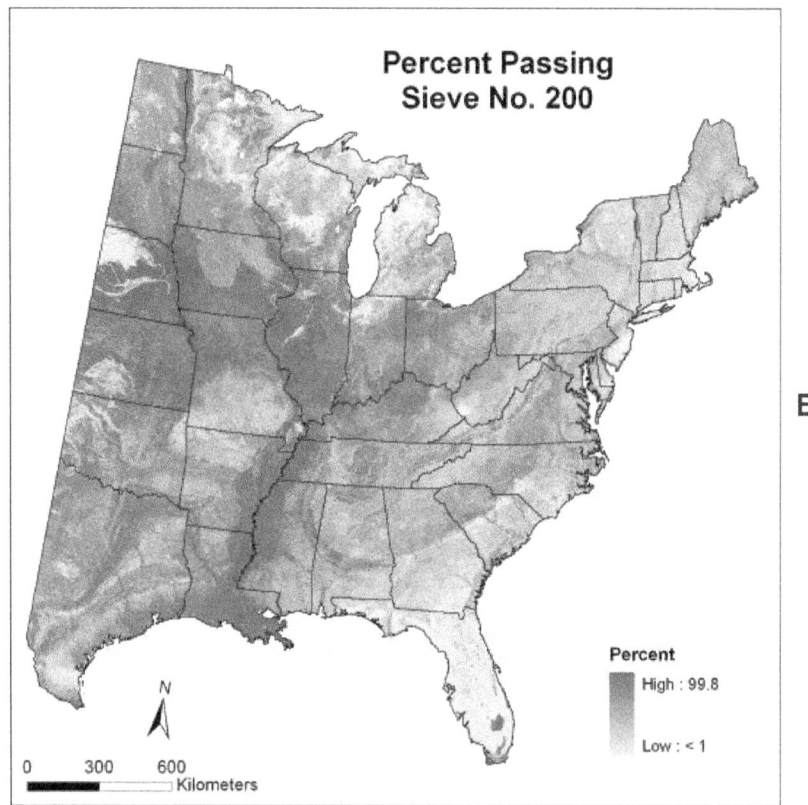

Figure 21.– Mean values of percentage of soil (A) passing sieve number 10 (number of 4-km grids: 283,267; mean percentage passing sieve: 88.8) and (B) passing sieve number 200 (number of 4-km grids: 283,286; mean percentage passing sieve: 60.0), a surrogate for soil texture (Iverson et al. 2008), in the eastern United States.

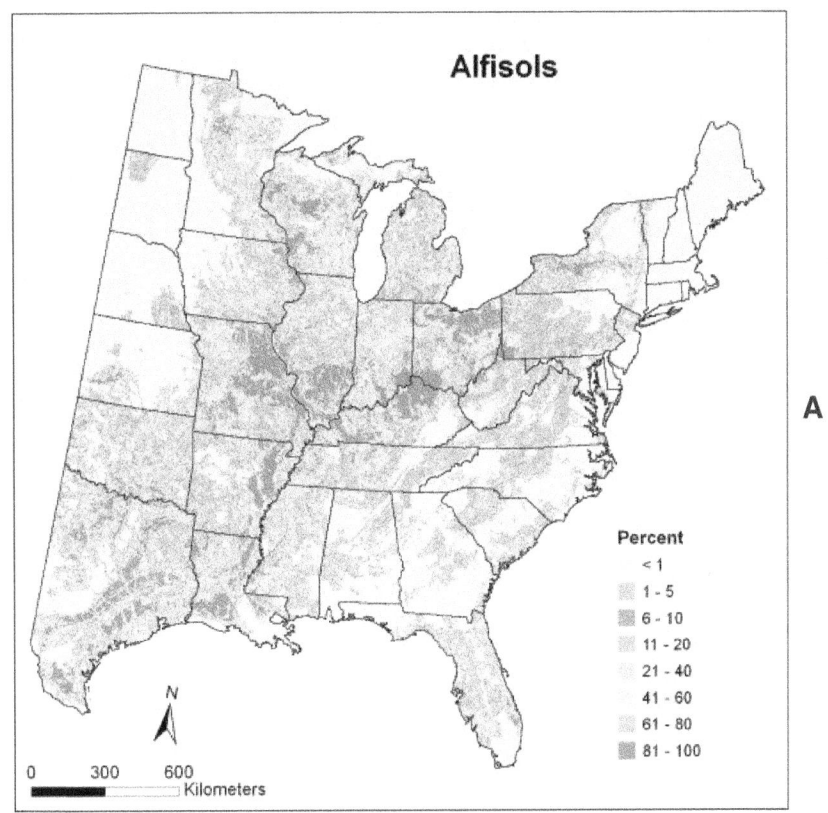

A

Figure 22.—Nine taxonomic orders of eastern U.S. soils by mean occupancy, based on SSURGO data. Mean occupancy of each order across the 37 states is as follows: (A) Alfisols (21.1%), (B) Aridisols (0.4%), (C) Entisols (9.1%), (D) Histosols (2.2%), (E) Inceptisols (11.3%), (F) Mollisols (26.3%), (G) Spodosols (5.9%), (H) Ultisols (20.1%), and (I) Vertisols (3.4%).

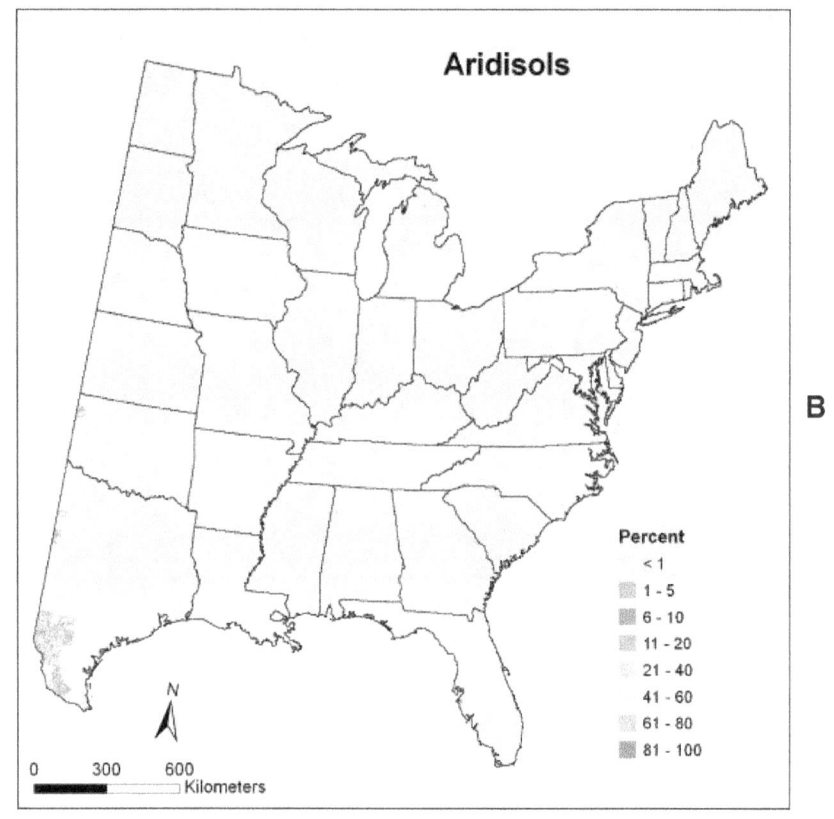

B

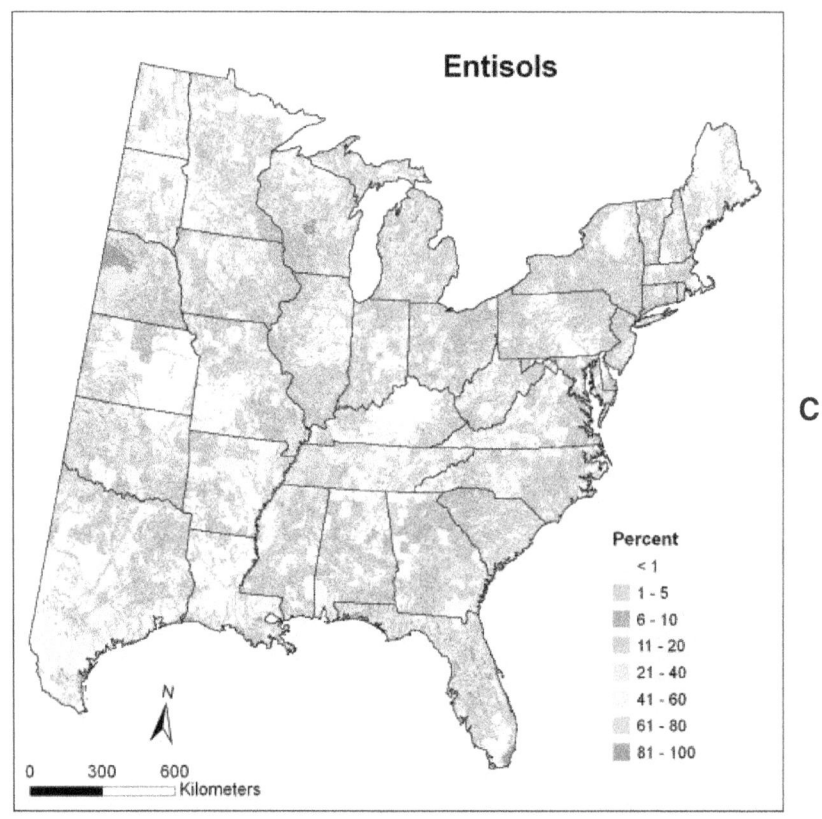

C

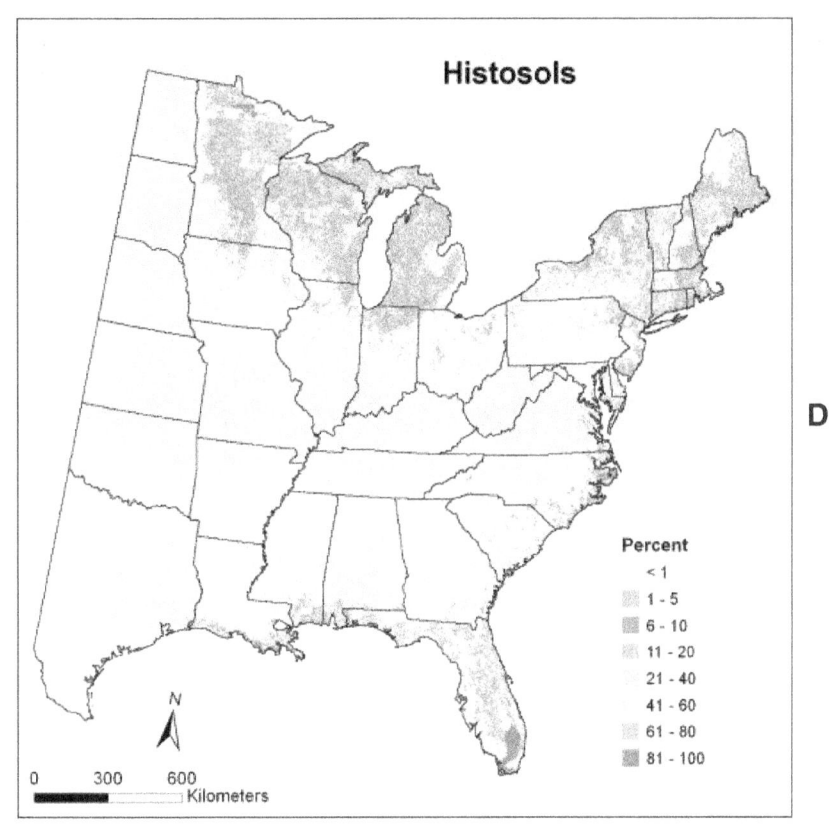

Histosols

D

Percent
< 1
1 - 5
6 - 10
11 - 20
21 - 40
41 - 60
61 - 80
81 - 100

0   300   600
Kilometers

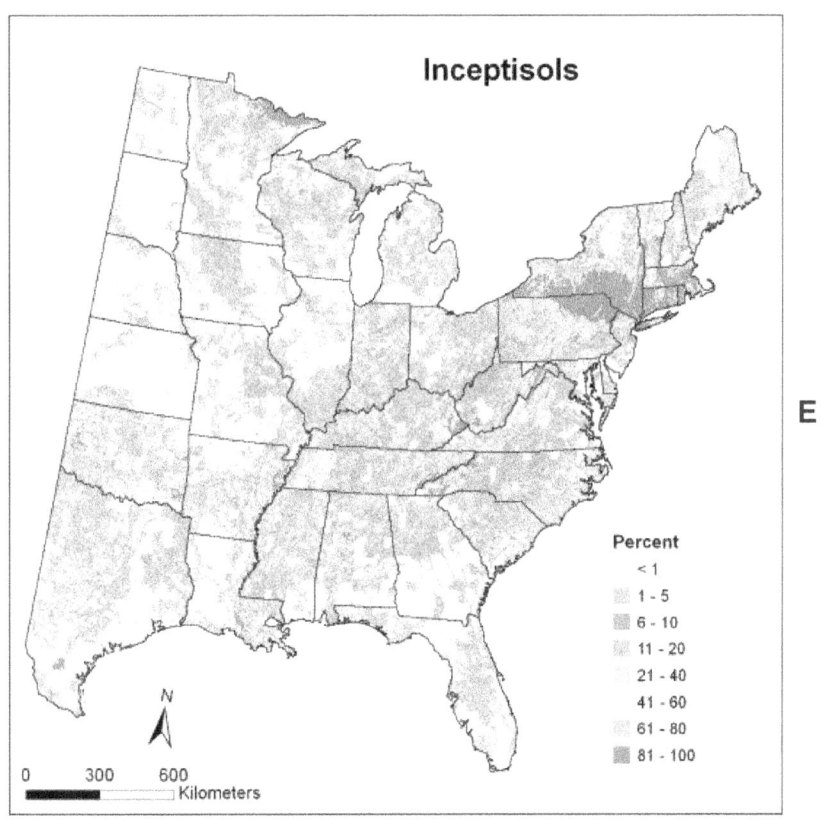

Inceptisols

E

Percent
< 1
1 - 5
6 - 10
11 - 20
21 - 40
41 - 60
61 - 80
81 - 100

0   300   600
Kilometers

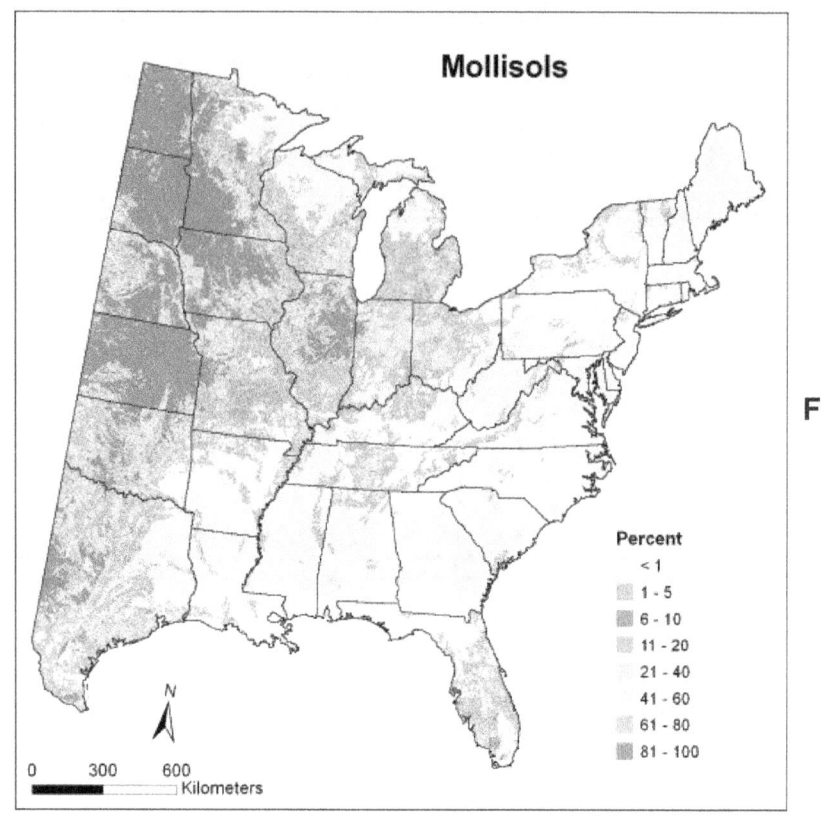

F

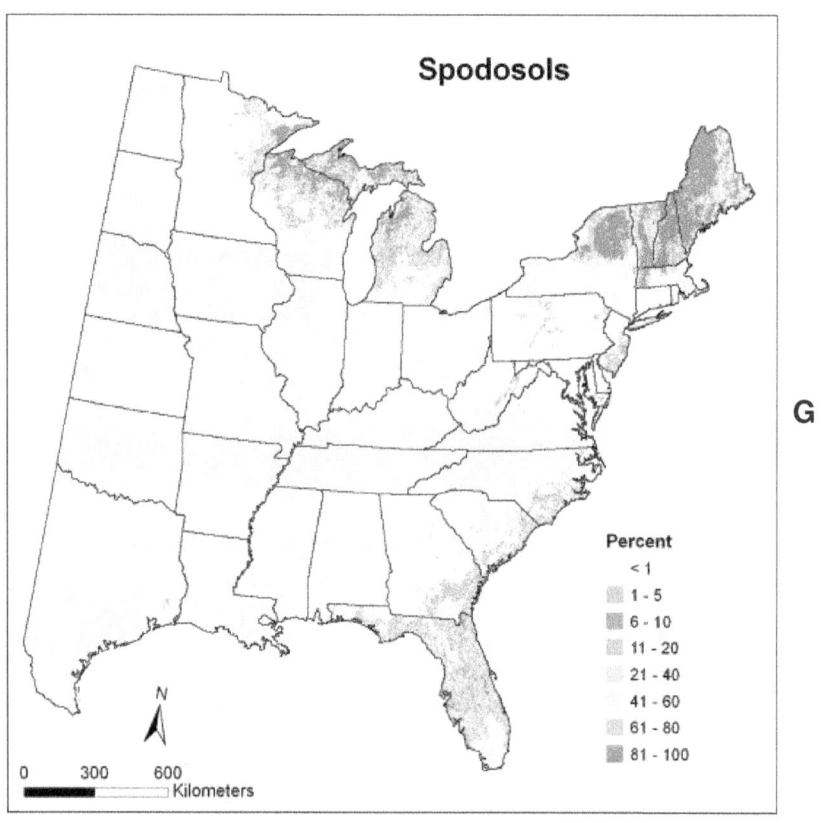

G

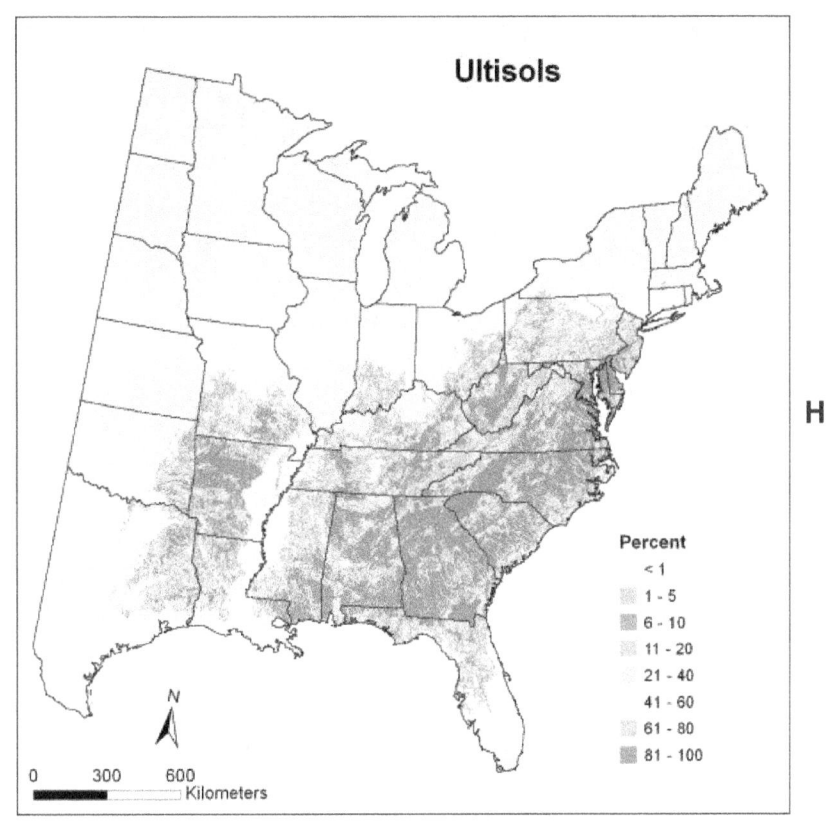

H

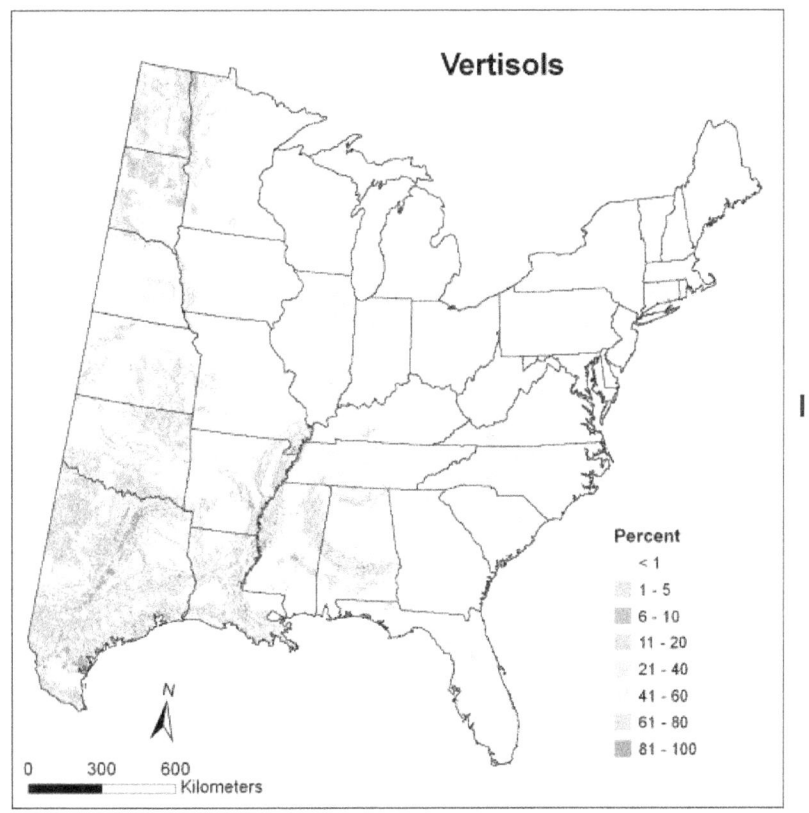

I

33

APPENDIX 3: STATE STATISTICS TABLES

Tables for each of the 37 states east of the 100th meridian were generated by running zonal statistics on the 30-m raster grids for 12 soil characteristics and properties. Taxonomic orders are reported as occupancy percentages within the state boundaries determined by area. Two area values are provided for each state, one obtained by the vector shapefile and the other derived from the number of 30-m grid cells used to calculate the statistics. Differences among these area values are due to the inclusion/exclusion rule used by the geoprocessor to determine which raster grids belong to each zone. Additionally, values for states intersected by the 100th meridian represent the area east of this line and are indicated by an asterisk (*).

Alabama

Area: 133,943.3 km^2 (shapefile feature)
       131,278.3 km^2 (processing area)

	MIN	MEAN	MAX	RANGE	STD	MEDIAN
Available water supply (cm)	0.19	20.68	44.84	44.65	5.40	21.45
Bulk density (g/cm)	0.15	1.53	1.78	1.63	0.09	1.54
Percent clay (<0.002 mm)	0.50	32.58	77	76.50	13.18	30.10
Forest productivity (ft^3/ac/yr)	0	143.31	186	186	26.63	157
Kffact	0.02	0.34	10.04	10.02	0.06	0.37
Organic matter (% by weight)	0.01	2.23	90	89.99	8.17	0.94
Permeability (cm/hr)	1	32.16	247	246	29.95	18
pH	2.10	5.44	8.30	6.20	0.70	5.30
Rock depth (cm)	25	159.97	201	176	45.06	163
Sieve no. 10 (%)	26	88.4	100	74	12.26	93
Sieve no. 200 (%)	2	54.9	97	95	16.69	54

Taxonomic orders (percent)
Area: 132,476.5 km^2 (processing area)

Alfisols	Aridisols	Entisols	Histosols	Inceptisols	Mollisols	Spodosols	Ultisols	Vertisols
5.29	0.00	6.47	0.53	11.63	1.05	0.02	71.53	3.47

Arkansas

Area: 137,045.4 km² (shapefile feature)
       134,125.4 km² (processing area)

	MIN	MEAN	MAX	RANGE	STD	MEDIAN
Available water supply (cm)	10.77	22.37	36.37	25.6	8.19	23.48
Bulk density (g/cm)	0.18	1.45	1.77	1.59	0.08	1.45
Percent clay (<0.002 mm)	0.4	33.46	75	74.6	14.94	28.1
Forest productivity (ft³/ac/yr)	0	113.49	186	186	26.15	114
Kffact	0.02	0.38	0.74	0.72	0.07	0.37
Organic matter (% by weight)	0.01	0.68	4.8	4.79	0.34	0.61
Permeability (cm/hr)	1	11.52	195	194	14.63	8
pH	2.1	5.53	8.3	6.2	0.80	5.3
Rock depth (cm)	18	157.90	201	183	51.05	201
Sieve no. 10 (%)	16	85.18	100	84	18.27	94
Sieve no. 200 (%)	5	65.74	99	94	21.13	66

Taxonomic orders (percent)
Area: 135,728.39 km² (processing area)

Alfisols	Aridisols	Entisols	Histosols	Inceptisols	Mollisols	Spodosols	Ultisols	Vertisols
27.53	0.00	4.91	0.00	12.26	1.68	0.00	50.72	2.91

Connecticut

Area: 12,889.4 km² (shapefile feature)
       12,646.3 km² (processing area)

	MIN	MEAN	MAX	RANGE	STD	MEDIAN
Available water supply (cm)	0.62	16.50	51.8	51.18	3.28	17.09
Bulk density (g/cm)	0.18	1.59	1.87	1.69	0.19	1.5
Percent clay (<0.002 mm)	0.8	11.25	35.4	34.6	5.66	11.6
Forest productivity (ft³/ac/yr)	0	129.05	143	143	23.16	129
Kffact	0.02	0.55	0.77	0.75	0.07	0.55
Organic matter (% by weight)	0.1	7.10	84.5	84.4	13.87	4.36
Permeability (cm/hr)	1	74.47	361	360	61.66	55
pH	2.9	5.97	8	5.1	0.67	5.5
Rock depth (cm)	2	84.88	201	199	37.69	77
Sieve no. 10 (%)	45	73.08	100	55	7.45	74
Sieve no. 200 (%)	11	38.10	96	85	12.77	36

Taxonomic orders (percent)
Area: 12,663.05 km² (processing area)

Alfisols	Aridisols	Entisols	Histosols	Inceptisols	Mollisols	Spodosols	Ultisols	Vertisols
0.00	0.00	13.68	2.90	83.21	0.21	0.00	0.00	0.00

Delaware

Area: 5,321.4 km² (shapefile feature)
       5,105 km² (processing area)

	MIN	MEAN	MAX	RANGE	STD	MEDIAN
Available water supply (cm)	7.5	22.35	60.13	52.63	7.64	21.02
Bulk density (g/cm)	0.3	1.52	1.84	1.54	0.21	1.61
Percent clay (<0.002 mm)	1	11.87	47.5	46.5	6.08	11.3
Forest productivity (ft³/ac/yr)	0	131.72	186	186	35.14	120
Kffact	0.02	0.31	0.73	0.71	0.12	0.28
Organic matter (% by weight)	0.02	3.71	71.23	71.21	10.53	0.67
Permeability (cm/hr)	1	93.40	600	599	96.17	63
pH	2.2	5.09	7.1	4.9	0.45	5
Rock depth (cm)	25	162.52	202	177	72.15	201
Sieve no. 10 (%)	36	95.23	100	64	5.62	95
Sieve no. 200 (%)	4	38.39	94	90	17.47	36

Taxonomic orders (percent)
Area: 5,132.15 km² (processing area)

Alfisols	Aridisols	Entisols	Histosols	Inceptisols	Mollisols	Spodosols	Ultisols	Vertisols
0.12	0.00	4.62	1.48	5.24	0.00	0.12	88.41	0.00

District of Columbia

Area: 171.1 km² (shapefile feature)
       154.9 km² (processing area)

	MIN	MEAN	MAX	RANGE	STD	MEDIAN
Available water supply (cm)	16.03	22.63	26.76	10.73	2.20	22.64
Bulk density (g/cm)	1.24	1.54	1.84	0.6	0.13	1.55
Percent clay (<0.002 mm)	2.9	23.98	47	44.1	10.90	23.5
Forest productivity (ft³/ac/yr)	57	114.45	186	129	24.87	114
Kffact	0.02	0.39	0.63	0.61	0.10	0.42
Organic matter (% by weight)	0.12	0.83	4.5	4.38	0.59	0.58
Permeability (cm/hr)	1	61.74	423	422	77.60	28
pH	2.2	4.96	8	5.8	0.39	5
Rock depth (cm)	25	94.70	202	177	86.08	25
Sieve no. 10 (%)	24	77.99	100	76	14.73	82
Sieve no. 200 (%)	10	44.46	83	73	14.91	44

Taxonomic orders (percent)
Area: 158.76 km² (processing area)

Alfisols	Aridisols	Entisols	Histosols	Inceptisols	Mollisols	Spodosols	Ultisols	Vertisols
0.39	0.00	7.96	0.00	8.91	0.12	0.00	82.61	0.00

Florida

Area: 144,558.7 km² (shapefile feature)
       138,143.4 km² (processing area)

	MIN	MEAN	MAX	RANGE	STD	MEDIAN
Available water supply (cm)	0.13	18.34	63.7	63.57	8.53	16.96
Bulk density (g/cm)	0.15	1.50	2.05	1.9	0.26	1.57
Percent clay (<0.002 mm)	0.4	15.10	85	84.6	11.82	13
Forest productivity (ft³/ac/yr)	0	134.40	186	186	38.62	143
Kffact	0.02	0.30	10.95	10.93	0.49	0.23
Organic matter (% by weight)	0.04	12.88	87.8	87.76	24.32	1.54
Permeability (cm/hr)	1	110.50	423	422	65.56	92
pH	2.1	6.12	8.5	6.4	0.95	5.9
Rock depth (cm)	15	123.07	201	186	74.01	143
Sieve no. 10 (%)	27	97.15	100	73	5.84	99
Sieve no. 200 (%)	1	22.33	100	99	21.32	14

Taxonomic orders (percent)
Area: 139,623.98 km² (processing area)

Alfisols	Aridisols	Entisols	Histosols	Inceptisols	Mollisols	Spodosols	Ultisols	Vertisols
12.50	0.00	20.95	11.83	3.56	5.79	25.04	20.28	0.03

Georgia

Area: 151,849.0 km² (shapefile feature)
       149,300.5 km² (processing area)

	MIN	MEAN	MAX	RANGE	STD	MEDIAN
Available water supply (cm)	2.57	19.61	63.7	61.13	3.66	20.07
Bulk density (g/cm)	0.15	1.47	2.02	1.87	0.11	1.49
Percent clay (<0.002 mm)	0.3	24.72	63.7	63.4	11.62	24.3
Forest productivity (ft³/ac/yr)	0	137.19	196	196	29.51	143
Kffact	0.02	0.26	8	7.98	0.07	0.28
Organic matter (% by weight)	0.01	0.97	69.5	69.49	3.21	0.43
Permeability (cm/hr)	1	27.33	247	246	27.73	13
pH	2.1	5.16	7.9	5.8	0.44	5
Rock depth (cm)	25	149.24	201	176	71.80	201
Sieve no. 10 (%)	25	91.96	100	75	8.09	95
Sieve no. 200 (%)	3	44.31	98	95	17.43	44

Taxonomic orders (percent)
Area: 150,807.89 km² (processing area)

Alfisols	Aridisols	Entisols	Histosols	Inceptisols	Mollisols	Spodosols	Ultisols	Vertisols
1.79	0.00	8.73	0.11	5.38	0.00	1.98	82.01	0.00

Illinois

Area: 145,817.7 km^2 (shapefile feature)

144,170.5 km^2 (processing area)

	MIN	MEAN	MAX	RANGE	STD	MEDIAN
Available water supply (cm)	8.01	27.59	59.53	51.52	4.63	28.52
Bulk density (g/cm)	0.15	1.47	2.16	2.01	0.11	1.47
Percent clay (<0.002mm)	0.7	28.26	67.1	66.4	7.41	28.3
Forest productivity (ft^3/ac/yr)	0	68.65	200	200	43.19	57
Kffact	0.02	0.42	0.75	0.73	0.08	0.43
Organic matter (% by weight)	0.02	1.50	85	84.98	4.69	0.99
Permeability (cm/hr)	1	11.13	423	422	21.95	9
pH	2.2	6.53	9.3	7.1	0.74	6.6
Rock depth (cm)	0	192.81	201	201	27.43	201
Sieve no. 10 (%)	29	96.12	100	71	6.19	98
Sieve no. 200 (%)	6	82.51	99	93	16.87	87

Taxonomic orders (percent)

Area: 144,754.16 km^2 (processing area)

Alfisols	Aridisols	Entisols	Histosols	Inceptisols	Mollisols	Spodosols	Ultisols	Vertisols
43.64	0.00	6.22	0.33	2.69	46.98	0.00	0.15	0.00

Indiana

Area: 94,278.2 km^2 (shapefile feature)

93,682.5 km^2 (processing area)

	MIN	MEAN	MAX	RANGE	STD	MEDIAN
Available water supply (cm)	10.27	24.73	54.38	44.11	6.16	25.01
Bulk density (g/cm)	0.15	1.56	1.89	1.74	0.15	1.59
Percent clay (<0.002 mm)	0.2	24.32	75.3	75.1	10.50	23.3
Forest productivity (ft^3/ac/yr)	0	92.04	200	200	30.65	86
Kffact	0.02	0.41	0.79	0.77	0.12	0.43
Organic matter (% by weight)	0.01	2.01	91.18	91.17	7.80	0.87
Permeability (cm/hr)	1	18.15	322	321	27.76	7
pH	2.1	6.46	8.1	6	0.90	6.9
Rock depth (cm)	25	164.58	201	176	41.77	201
Sieve no. 10 (%)	24	92.58	100	76	8.92	95
Sieve no. 200 (%)	7	66.37	100	93	22.01	73

Taxonomic orders (percent)

Area: 94,026.22 km^2 (processing area)

Alfisols	Aridisols	Entisols	Histosols	Inceptisols	Mollisols	Spodosols	Ultisols	Vertisols
55.51	0.00	5.86	1.34	8.65	23.97	0.00	4.66	0.00

Iowa

Area: 145,711.1 km^2 (shapefile feature)

144,896.9 km^2 (processing area)

	MIN	MEAN	MAX	RANGE	STD	MEDIAN
Available water supply (cm)	11.1	28.69	33.16	22.01	2.95	28.14
Bulk density (g/cm)	0.15	1.45	1.78	1.63	0.11	1.45
Percent clay (<0.002 mm)	0.7	30.46	66	65.3	8.32	30.5
Forest productivity (ft^3/ac/yr)	0	51.19	200	200	24.93	43
Kffact	0.02	0.38	0.73	0.71	0.06	0.38
Organic matter (% by weight)	0.06	2.67	84.5	84.44	4.22	1.46
Permeability (cm/hr)	1	14.41	361	360	26.28	9
pH	2.1	6.73	8.3	6.2	0.68	6.6
Rock depth (cm)	0	178.95	201	201	50.45	201
Sieve no. 10 (%)	39	96.07	100	61	5.26	98
Sieve no. 200 (%)	3	78.91	98	95	19.515	86

Taxonomic orders (percent)

Area: 145,248.64 km^2 (processing area)

Alfisols	Aridisols	Entisols	Histosols	Inceptisols	Mollisols	Spodosols	Ultisols	Vertisols
20.89	0.00	6.95	0.26	4.15	67.47	0.00	0.00	0.27

Kansas*

Area: 153,342.9 km^2 (shapefile feature)

152,448.9 km^2 (processing area)

	MIN	MEAN	MAX	RANGE	STD	MEDIAN
Available water supply (cm)	11.47	24.08	37.76	26.29	5.23	24.4
Bulk density (g/cm)	0.31	1.44	2.09	1.78	0.09	1.44
Percent clay (<0.002 mm)	0.5	35.88	70.4	69.9	12.06	38
Forest productivity (ft^3/ac/yr)	0	63.95	157	157	34.87	57
Kffact	0.02	0.42	0.77	0.75	0.10	0.43
Organic matter (% by weight)	0.03	1.48	7.42	7.39	0.77	1.34
Permeability (cm/hr)	1	12.27	201	200	19.34	8
pH	2.7	7.29	8.6	5.9	0.54	7.3
Rock depth (cm)	31	131.73	201	170	52.44	127
Sieve no. 10 (%)	29	95.82	100	71	8.11	99
Sieve no. 200 (%)	8	79.73	99	91	19.61	88

Taxonomic orders (percent)

Area: 152,866.76 km^2 (processing area)

Alfisols	Aridisols	Entisols	Histosols	Inceptisols	Mollisols	Spodosols	Ultisols	Vertisols
6.44	0.00	3.53	0.00	2.28	87.02	0.00	0.06	0.66

Kentucky

Area: 104,428.7 km^2 (shapefile feature)

103,227.8 km^2 (processing area)

	MIN	MEAN	MAX	RANGE	STD	MEDIAN
Available water supply (cm)	8.17	20.07	38.31	30.14	6.49	17.98
Bulk density (g/cm)	0.15	1.46	1.75	1.6	0.08	1.46
Percent clay (<0.002 mm)	0.3	32.83	68.1	67.8	10.67	29.1
Forest productivity (ft^3/ac/yr)	0	111.84	429	429	32.31	114
Kffact	0.02	0.39	0.77	0.75	0.09	0.37
Organic matter (% by weight)	0.01	0.79	10.39	10.38	0.53	0.62
Permeability (cm/hr)	1	15.94	282	281	21.64	9
pH	2.1	5.66	8.1	6	0.78	5.4
Rock depth (cm)	0	126.89	201	201	41.89	102
Sieve no. 10 (%)	15	82.04	100	85	14.02	85
Sieve no. 200 (%)	4	69.84	98	94	17.47	74

Taxonomic orders (percent)

Area: 103,484.27 km^2 (processing area)

Alfisols	Aridisols	Entisols	Histosols	Inceptisols	Mollisols	Spodosols	Ultisols	Vertisols
43.67	0.00	3.29	0.00	21.13	3.29	0.00	28.55	0.08

Louisiana

Area: 118,714.2 km^2 (shapefile feature)

110,721.7 km^2 (processing area)

	MIN	MEAN	MAX	RANGE	STD	MEDIAN
Available water supply (cm)	1.28	29.29	57.22	55.94	5.55	29.7
Bulk density (g/cm)	0.15	1.31	1.73	1.58	0.38	1.46
Percent clay (<0.002 mm)	0.2	38.61	78.4	78.2	19.45	32
Forest productivity (ft^3/ac/yr)	0	123.62	200	200	41.92	129
Kffact	0.02	0.38	0.64	0.62	0.09	0.37
Organic matter (% by weight)	0.01	4.09	51.29	51.28	9.86	0.81
Permeability (cm/hr)	1	13.57	141	140	20.84	5
pH	2.1	5.99	8.1	6	1.01	5.6
Rock depth (cm)	5	177.42	201	196	56.42	201
Sieve no. 10 (%)	41	97.80	100	59	4.87	100
Sieve no. 200 (%)	5	80.85	98	93	16.50	87

Taxonomic orders (percent)

Area: 114,887.65 km^2 (processing area)

Alfisols	Aridisols	Entisols	Histosols	Inceptisols	Mollisols	Spodosols	Ultisols	Vertisols
36.10	0.00	7.09	7.46	10.42	1.49	0.00	21.81	15.63

Maine

Area: 83,302.7 km² (shapefile feature)
         79,644.2 km² (processing area)

	MIN	MEAN	MAX	RANGE	STD	MEDIAN
Available water supply (cm)	0.34	19.26	57.75	57.41	4.57	18.77
Bulk density (g/cm)	0.17	1.37	1.84	1.67	0.30	1.47
Percent clay (<0.002 mm)	0.2	12.55	45.7	45.5	8.47	9.6
Forest productivity (ft³/ac/yr)	0	117.41	172	172	29.52	129
Kffact	0.02	0.34	0.77	0.75	0.10	0.36
Organic matter (% by weight)	0.05	7.51	100	99.95	14.38	3.9
Permeability (cm/hr)	1	21.29	141	140	29.56	9
pH	2.1	5.42	7.9	5.8	0.57	5.4
Rock depth (cm)	14	83.39	201	187	41.15	77
Sieve no. 10 (%)	20	76.66	100	80	10.53	76
Sieve no. 200 (%)	2	51.84	100	98	16.91	54

Taxonomic orders (percent)
Area: 80,249.03 km² (processing area)

Alfisols	Aridisols	Entisols	Histosols	Inceptisols	Mollisols	Spodosols	Ultisols	Vertisols
0.00	0.00	1.10	3.26	16.23	0.00	79.41	0.00	0.00

Maryland

Area: 25,226.9 km² (shapefile feature)
         24,098 km² (processing area)

	MIN	MEAN	MAX	RANGE	STD	MEDIAN
Available water supply (cm)	0.33	21.00	66.47	66.14	6.81	22
Bulk density (g/cm)	0.16	1.47	1.94	1.78	0.17	1.47
Percent clay (<0.002 mm)	0.3	20.86	66	65.7	9.61	20.2
Forest productivity (ft³/ac/yr)	0	107.61	186	186	27.80	114
Kffact	0.02	0.40	0.77	0.75	0.10	0.43
Organic matter (% by weight)	0.04	3.00	71.23	71.19	9.55	0.87
Permeability (cm/hr)	1	38.21	423	422	48.38	21
pH	2.1	5.06	8	5.9	0.62	5
Rock depth (cm)	25	165.87	241	216	61.05	201
Sieve no. 10 (%)	2	80.52	100	98	14.91	84
Sieve no. 200 (%)	2	48.02	93	91	15.80	49

Taxonomic orders (percent)
Area: 24,379.41 km² (processing area)

Alfisols	Aridisols	Entisols	Histosols	Inceptisols	Mollisols	Spodosols	Ultisols	Vertisols
9.85	0.00	5.02	1.67	11.76	0.11	0.74	70.86	0.00

Massachusetts

Area: 21,167.4 km² (shapefile feature)
       19,920.8 km² (processing area)

	MIN	MEAN	MAX	RANGE	STD	MEDIAN
Available water supply (cm)	3	14.62	60	57	4.43	15.08
Bulk density (g/cm)	0.15	1.35	1.92	1.77	0.30	1.37
Percent clay (<0.002 mm)	0.2	6.81	44.2	44	4.90	6.5
Forest productivity (ft³/ac/yr)	0	100.81	157	157	31.03	114
Kffact	0.02	0.40	0.78	0.76	0.15	0.47
Organic matter (% by weight)	0.01	7.43	90	89.99	17.76	2.25
Permeability (cm/hr)	1	47.38	361	360	45.11	23
pH	2.1	5.12	8	5.9	0.52	5.3
Rock depth (cm)	0	62.99	201	201	47.67	38
Sieve no. 10 (%)	26	74.65	100	74	12.01	75
Sieve no. 200 (%)	2	32.72	100	98	14.71	36

Taxonomic orders (percent)
Area: 20,498.07 km² (processing area)

Alfisols	Aridisols	Entisols	Histosols	Inceptisols	Mollisols	Spodosols	Ultisols	Vertisols
0.00	0.00	11.30	5.54	64.76	0.05	18.10	0.25	0.00

Michigan

Area: 149,963.2 km² (shapefile feature)
       145,895.8 km² (processing area)

	MIN	MEAN	MAX	RANGE	STD	MEDIAN
Available water supply (cm)	0.99	20.85	65.12	64.13	9.15	20.95
Bulk density (g/cm)	0.15	1.56	1.94	1.79	0.18	1.58
Percent clay (<0.002 mm)	0.3	18.10	72.5	72.2	12.20	15.8
Forest productivity (ft³/ac/yr)	0	88.53	200	200	33.09	86
Kffact	0.02	0.31	0.77	0.75	0.10	0.32
Organic matter (% by weight)	0.05	15.03	140.78	140.73	28.51	1.26
Permeability (cm/hr)	1	66.81	373	372	40.73	85
pH	2.1	6.87	8.3	6.2	0.75	7
Rock depth (cm)	5	170.49	201	196	59.59	201
Sieve no. 10 (%)	25	89.06	100	75	8.32	91
Sieve no. 200 (%)	2	40.21	97	95	24.37	35

Taxonomic orders (percent)
Area: 147,392.08 km² (processing area)

Alfisols	Aridisols	Entisols	Histosols	Inceptisols	Mollisols	Spodosols	Ultisols	Vertisols
30.37	0.00	11.68	9.47	6.00	9.14	33.34	0.00	0.00

Minnesota

Area: 218,914.9 km^2 (shapefile feature)

206,723.7 km^2 (processing area)

	MIN	MEAN	MAX	RANGE	STD	MEDIAN
Available water supply (cm)	3.31	26.23	77.69	74.38	12.69	25.92
Bulk density (g/cm)	0.15	1.41	1.89	1.74	0.34	1.49
Percent clay (<0.002 mm)	0.5	20.22	74.4	73.9	13.54	20
Forest productivity (ft^3/ac/yr)	0	62.45	143	143	22.38	65
Kffact	0.02	0.32	0.77	0.75	0.09	0.32
Organic matter (% by weight)	0.03	10.02	98	97.97	21.74	1.64
Permeability (cm/hr)	1	37.21	423	422	46.15	12
pH	2.2	6.92	8.1	5.9	0.89	7
Rock depth (cm)	0	188.97	201	201	34.86	201
Sieve no. 10 (%)	22	90.04	100	78	10.35	93
Sieve no. 200 (%)	0	56.77	100	100	25.96	63

Taxonomic orders (percent)

Area: 212,091.66 km^2 (processing area)

Alfisols	Aridisols	Entisols	Histosols	Inceptisols	Mollisols	Spodosols	Ultisols	Vertisols
18.09	0.00	6.06	10.57	11.68	47.29	4.43	0.00	1.87

Mississippi

Area: 123,332.6 km^2 (shapefile feature)

121,132 km^2 (processing area)

	MIN	MEAN	MAX	RANGE	STD	MEDIAN
Available water supply (cm)	1.28	26.86	41.58	40.3	4.16	26.53
Bulk density (g/cm)	0.15	1.52	1.7	1.55	0.08	1.51
Percent clay (<0.002 mm)	0.5	29.35	77	76.5	14.83	24.2
Forest productivity (ft^3/ac/yr)	0	141.05	229	229	31.44	157
Kffact	0.02	0.41	7	6.98	0.24	0.37
Organic matter (% by weight)	0.01	1.03	70	69.99	3.71	0.57
Permeability (cm/hr)	1	15.63	247	246	18.51	9
pH	2.1	5.51	8.1	6	0.80	5.3
Rock depth (cm)	31	190.55	201	170	33.83	201
Sieve no. 10 (%)	36	95.57	100	64	6.11	98
Sieve no. 200 (%)	2	70.55	100	98	19.88	71

Taxonomic orders (percent)

Area: 122,561.15 km^2 (processing area)

Alfisols	Aridisols	Entisols	Histosols	Inceptisols	Mollisols	Spodosols	Ultisols	Vertisols
25.33	0.00	9.74	0.65	12.64	0.45	0.00	41.30	9.90

Missouri

Area: 180,868.4 km^2 (shapefile feature)
179,294.2 km^2 (processing area)

	MIN	MEAN	MAX	RANGE	STD	MEDIAN
Available water supply (cm)	9.93	21.28	36.37	26.44	6.31	21.67
Bulk density (g/cm)	0.15	1.45	2.09	1.94	0.08	1.46
Percent clay (<0.002 mm)	0.5	38.53	80.9	80.4	12.23	38.2
Forest productivity (ft^3/ac/yr)	0	73.54	186	186	33.92	57
Kffact	0.02	0.44	0.79	0.77	0.10	0.43
Organic matter (% by weight)	0.03	1.12	7.34	7.31	0.84	0.93
Permeability (cm/hr)	1	9.61	212	211	20.84	4
pH	2.1	6.00	8.3	6.2	0.77	6
Rock depth (cm)	18	132.19	201	183	50.14	132
Sieve no. 10 (%)	10	80.35	100	90	21.89	91
Sieve no. 200 (%)	2	67.05	100	98	23.16	70

Taxonomic orders (percent)
Area: 180,071.16 km^2 (processing area)

Alfisols	Aridisols	Entisols	Histosols	Inceptisols	Mollisols	Spodosols	Ultisols	Vertisols
50.79	0.00	4.93	0.00	3.38	23.71	0.00	15.72	1.48

Nebraska*

Area: 106,565.3 km^2 (shapefile feature)
105,877.9 km^2 (processing area)

	MIN	MEAN	MAX	RANGE	STD	MEDIAN
Available water supply (cm)	7.75	24.41	33.34	25.59	7.54	28.08
Bulk density (g/cm)	0.17	1.43	1.96	1.79	0.14	1.39
Percent clay (<0.002 mm)	0.5	23.80	66.4	65.9	12.30	25.2
Forest productivity (ft^3/ac/yr)	0	46.06	157	157	17.95	43
Kffact	0.02	0.39	0.77	0.75	0.11	0.43
Organic matter (% by weight)	0.04	1.25	30.02	29.98	0.95	1.01
Permeability (cm/hr)	1	34.08	423	422	53.43	9
pH	2.4	7.17	9	6.6	0.54	7
Rock depth (cm)	31	194.94	201	170	25.80	201
Sieve no. 10 (%)	37	98.30	100	63	4.62	100
Sieve no. 200 (%)	5	72.86	98	93	32.51	92

Taxonomic orders (percent)
Area: 106,256.02 km^2 (processing area)

Alfisols	Aridisols	Entisols	Histosols	Inceptisols	Mollisols	Spodosols	Ultisols	Vertisols
3.03	0.00	29.85	0.00	1.51	65.50	0.00	0.00	0.11

New Hampshire

Area: 23,982.6 km^2 (shapefile feature)
        22,937.3 km^2 (processing area)

	MIN	MEAN	MAX	RANGE	STD	MEDIAN
Available water supply (cm)	0.38	14.73	59.67	59.29	2.88	14.25
Bulk density (g/cm)	0.16	1.53	2.02	1.86	0.22	1.63
Percent clay (<0.002 mm)	0.2	7.00	44.2	44	5.21	6.5
Forest productivity (ft^3/ac/yr)	0	122.85	172	172	31.32	129
Kffact	0.02	0.34	0.77	0.75	0.09	0.37
Organic matter (% by weight)	0.05	21.72	100	99.95	30.63	5
Permeability (cm/hr)	1	49.41	390	389	40.96	35
pH	2.1	5.41	7	4.9	0.46	5.4
Rock depth (cm)	25	78.53	201	176	30.30	77
Sieve no. 10 (%)	2	76.52	100	98	10.43	78
Sieve no. 200 (%)	2	36.95	93	91	12.75	39

Taxonomic orders (percent)
Area: 23,539.56 km^2 (processing area)

Alfisols	Aridisols	Entisols	Histosols	Inceptisols	Mollisols	Spodosols	Ultisols	Vertisols
0.00	0.00	5.69	4.19	25.95	0.00	64.17	0.00	0.00

New Jersey

Area: 19,444.7 km^2 (shapefile feature)
        18,972.1 km^2 (processing area)

	MIN	MEAN	MAX	RANGE	STD	MEDIAN
Available water supply (cm)	0.75	17.57	64.63	63.88	7.22	15.44
Bulk density (g/cm)	0.16	1.51	2.02	1.86	0.19	1.55
Percent clay (<0.002 mm)	0.5	14.65	47.5	47	9.71	12.5
Forest productivity (ft^3/ac/yr)	0	101.53	157	157	23.65	114
Kffact	0.02	0.34	0.75	0.73	0.09	0.32
Organic matter (% by weight)	0.03	7.12	85	84.97	15.63	2.01
Permeability (cm/hr)	1	56.19	705	704	46.76	56
pH	2.1	5.27	7.5	5.4	0.61	5.3
Rock depth (cm)	25	123.32	217	192	72.75	143
Sieve no. 10 (%)	2	82.81	100	98	14.49	88
Sieve no. 200 (%)	2	35.80	100	98	21.05	29

Taxonomic orders (percent)
Area: 19,041.75 km^2 (processing area)

Alfisols	Aridisols	Entisols	Histosols	Inceptisols	Mollisols	Spodosols	Ultisols	Vertisols
9.12	0.00	15.06	4.19	16.20	0.26	5.84	49.33	0.00

New York

Area: 125,777.2 km^2 (shapefile feature)
  121,363 km^2 (processing area)

	MIN	MEAN	MAX	RANGE	STD	MEDIAN
Available water supply (cm)	1.33	14.72	60	58.67	6.58	12.96
Bulk density (g/cm)	0.15	1.43	1.87	1.72	0.23	1.47
Percent clay (<0.002 mm)	0.2	15.00	75	74.8	10.46	12
Forest productivity (ft^3/ac/yr)	0	89.90	200	200	39.79	86
Kffact	0.02	0.34	0.78	0.76	0.12	0.31
Organic matter (% by weight)	0.01	4.78	100	99.99	12.81	1.42
Permeability (cm/hr)	1	22.49	399	398	39.31	7
pH	2.1	5.88	8.1	6	0.83	5.6
Rock depth (cm)	18	98.46	201	183	55.96	77
Sieve no. 10 (%)	20	73.63	100	80	15.92	73
Sieve no. 200 (%)	2	44.88	100	98	18.46	44

Taxonomic orders (percent)
Area: 122,744.53 km^2 (processing area)

Alfisols	Aridisols	Entisols	Histosols	Inceptisols	Mollisols	Spodosols	Ultisols	Vertisols
17.90	0.00	5.73	2.36	53.03	0.34	20.10	0.53	0.00

North Carolina

Area: 127,034.3 km^2 (shapefile feature)
  124,272 km^2 (processing area)

	MIN	MEAN	MAX	RANGE	STD	MEDIAN
Available water supply (cm)	3	20.84	52.5	49.5	6.12	20.38
Bulk density (g/cm)	0.15	1.43	2.02	1.87	0.17	1.44
Percent clay (<0.002 mm)	0.3	23.97	58.4	58.1	10.35	24.8
Forest productivity (ft^3/ac/yr)	0	130.38	220	220	28.28	129
Kffact	0.02	0.32	0.78	0.76	0.09	0.31
Organic matter (% by weight)	0.02	2.70	95.08	95.06	7.64	0.66
Permeability (cm/hr)	1	25.08	212	211	24.35	14
pH	2.1	5.13	8	5.9	0.60	5
Rock depth (cm)	25	127.98	201	176	70.88	127
Sieve no. 10 (%)	2	90.14	100	98	9.17	93
Sieve no. 200 (%)	2	49.05	97	95	17.00	49

Taxonomic orders (percent)
Area: 125,603.93 km^2 (processing area)

Alfisols	Aridisols	Entisols	Histosols	Inceptisols	Mollisols	Spodosols	Ultisols	Vertisols
4.70	0.00	4.20	4.23	14.92	0.02	1.74	70.19	0.00

North Dakota*

Area: 79,451.8 km² (shapefile feature)
         79,046.1 km² (processing area)

	MIN	MEAN	MAX	RANGE	STD	MEDIAN
Available water supply (cm)	5.36	24.19	30.06	24.7	4.05	25.74
Bulk density (g/cm)	0.15	1.47	1.64	1.49	0.06	1.46
Percent clay (<0.002 mm)	1.7	34.62	71.4	69.7	10.50	39.7
Forest productivity (ft³/ac/yr)	0	35.72	72	72	12.11	29
Kffact	0.02	0.40	0.55	0.53	0.05	0.43
Organic matter (% by weight)	0.21	3.45	85	84.79	3.32	3.34
Permeability (cm/hr)	1	98.32	374	373	111.55	49
pH	2.2	7.93	9	6.8	0.16	7.9
Rock depth (cm)	10	190.10	201	191	38.78	201
Sieve no. 10 (%)	40	92.74	100	60	7.44	94
Sieve no. 200 (%)	9	63.23	96	87	17.49	66

Taxonomic orders (percent)
Area: 79,106.19 km² (processing area)

Alfisols	Aridisols	Entisols	Histosols	Inceptisols	Mollisols	Spodosols	Ultisols	Vertisols
0.27	0.00	1.89	0.00	0.66	91.48	0.00	0.00	5.70

Ohio

Area: 106,694.2 km² (shapefile feature)
         105,627.1 km² (processing area)

	MIN	MEAN	MAX	RANGE	STD	MEDIAN
Available water supply (cm)	5.81	20.66	57.52	51.71	3.97	20.46
Bulk density (g/cm)	0.18	1.53	1.94	1.76	0.12	1.54
Percent clay (<0.002 mm)	1.5	30.27	70.6	69.1	10.02	28.7
Forest productivity (ft³/ac/yr)	0	91.68	214	214	34.73	86
Kffact	0.02	0.39	0.78	0.76	0.09	0.38
Organic matter (% by weight)	0.05	1.06	86.73	86.68	3.76	0.72
Permeability (cm/hr)	1	11.41	373	372	21.92	4
pH	2.2	6.38	8.3	6.1	0.86	6.6
Rock depth (cm)	25	154.19	202	177	52.56	158
Sieve no. 10 (%)	9	83.31	100	91	13.88	88
Sieve no. 200 (%)	2	67.68	96	94	16.42	71

Taxonomic orders (percent)
Area: 106,279.12 km² (processing area)

Alfisols	Aridisols	Entisols	Histosols	Inceptisols	Mollisols	Spodosols	Ultisols	Vertisols
65.11	0.00	5.59	0.28	10.38	11.16	0.00	7.48	0.00

Oklahoma*

Area: 166,321.1 km^2 (shapefile feature)
163,844.3 km^2 (processing area)

	MIN	MEAN	MAX	RANGE	STD	MEDIAN
Available water supply (cm)	4.58	20.47	37.8	33.22	7.27	21.72
Bulk density (g/cm)	0.15	1.65	2.09	1.94	0.17	1.6
Percent clay (<0.002 mm)	0.3	35.29	73	72.7	11.09	38.7
Forest productivity (ft^3/ac/yr)	0	86.89	172	172	31.43	100
Kffact	0.02	0.40	0.78	0.76	0.07	0.42
Organic matter (% by weight)	0.01	1.07	4.5	4.49	0.54	0.98
Permeability (cm/hr)	1	25.81	423	422	33.73	17
pH	2.2	7.05	8.5	6.3	0.96	7.3
Rock depth (cm)	0	136.72	201	201	49.00	127
Sieve no. 10 (%)	25	92.01	100	75	12.50	97
Sieve no. 200 (%)	2	65.40	98	96	20.00	70

Taxonomic orders (percent)
Area: 164,375.47 km^2 (processing area)

Alfisols	Aridisols	Entisols	Histosols	Inceptisols	Mollisols	Spodosols	Ultisols	Vertisols
22.63	0.05	9.00	0.00	15.18	40.48	0.00	9.03	3.63

Pennsylvania

Area: 117,485.0 km^2 (shapefile feature)
116,549.7 km^2 (processing area)

	MIN	MEAN	MAX	RANGE	STD	MEDIAN
Available water supply (cm)	3.55	14.94	36.1	32.55	4.79	13.85
Bulk density (g/cm)	0.15	1.45	2.02	1.87	0.13	1.45
Percent clay (<0.002 mm)	0.3	22.50	63	62.7	7.44	23.1
Forest productivity (ft^3/ac/yr)	0	85.20	196	196	30.23	86
Kffact	0.02	0.38	0.77	0.75	0.11	0.37
Organic matter (% by weight)	0.01	1.15	90	89.99	5.27	0.68
Permeability (cm/hr)	1	20.98	423	422	26.11	9
pH	2.1	5.40	7.9	5.8	0.70	5.3
Rock depth (cm)	25	143.84	217	192	43.31	153
Sieve no. 10 (%)	2	66.51	100	98	14.03	65
Sieve no. 200 (%)	2	49.00	92	90	15.07	47

Taxonomic orders (percent)
Area: 117,026.51 km^2 (processing area)

Alfisols	Aridisols	Entisols	Histosols	Inceptisols	Mollisols	Spodosols	Ultisols	Vertisols
17.79	0.00	3.75	0.19	42.38	0.15	0.26	35.49	0.00

Rhode Island

Area: 2,706.3 km² (shapefile feature)
        2,589 km² (processing area)

	MIN	MEAN	MAX	RANGE	STD	MEDIAN
Available water supply (cm)	0.36	16.16	51.8	51.44	6.29	16.66
Bulk density (g/cm)	0.18	1.63	1.92	1.74	0.16	1.69
Percent clay (<0.002 mm)	0.5	6.49	35	34.5	2.04	7.5
Forest productivity (ft³/ac/yr)	0	131.81	143	143	21.76	143
Kffact	0.02	0.53	0.78	0.76	0.09	0.55
Organic matter (% by weight)	0.25	8.37	84.5	84.25	14.26	4
Permeability (cm/hr)	2	91.68	361	359	36.45	112
pH	2.6	5.62	7.4	4.8	0.21	5.5
Rock depth (cm)	2	66.23	201	199	42.44	77
Sieve no. 10 (%)	26	69.87	98	72	7.65	68
Sieve no. 200 (%)	2	32.35	95	93	12.55	31

Taxonomic orders (percent)
Area: 2,603.69 km² (processing area)

Alfisols	Aridisols	Entisols	Histosols	Inceptisols	Mollisols	Spodosols	Ultisols	Vertisols
0.00	0.00	12.37	4.06	83.57	0.00	0.00	0.00	0.00

South Carolina

Area: 79,946.7 km² (shapefile feature)
        78,378.3 km² (processing area)

	MIN	MEAN	MAX	RANGE	STD	MEDIAN
Available water supply (cm)	1.82	19.18	44.87	43.05	4.58	19.92
Bulk density (g/cm)	0.15	1.46	1.85	1.7	0.11	1.44
Percent clay (<0.002 mm)	0.4	27.67	63	62.6	12.82	27.5
Forest productivity (ft³/ac/yr)	0	121.73	198	198	24.41	114
Kffact	0.02	0.27	0.68	0.66	0.07	0.28
Organic matter (% by weight)	0.02	1.12	69.5	69.48	3.53	0.4
Permeability (cm/hr)	1	28.69	180	179	28.43	14
pH	2.1	5.16	8.1	6	0.55	5
Rock depth (cm)	25	171.25	201	176	54.93	201
Sieve no. 10 (%)	37	95.93	100	63	4.89	97
Sieve no. 200 (%)	3	49.31	97	94	20.54	47

Taxonomic orders (percent)
Area: 78,649.22 km² (processing area)

Alfisols	Aridisols	Entisols	Histosols	Inceptisols	Mollisols	Spodosols	Ultisols	Vertisols
8.25	0.00	10.79	0.63	7.46	0.30	1.86	70.71	0.00

South Dakota*

Area: 94,068.0 km² (shapefile feature)
          92,921.5 km² (processing area)

	MIN	MEAN	MAX	RANGE	STD	MEDIAN
Available water supply (cm)	6.9	24.97	32.21	25.31	5.02	26.65
Bulk density (g/cm)	0.43	1.48	2.18	1.75	0.09	1.48
Percent clay (<0.002 mm)	0.5	40.21	67.5	67	10.01	40.5
Forest productivity (ft³/ac/yr)	0	66.77	157	157	45.56	43
Kffact	0.02	0.41	0.61	0.59	0.04	0.43
Organic matter (% by weight)	0.13	2.45	10	9.87	0.84	2.36
Permeability (cm/hr)	1	34.12	410	409	57.11	9
pH	2.6	7.94	9	6.4	0.25	7.9
Rock depth (cm)	31	186.11	201	170	40.28	201
Sieve no. 10 (%)	2	94.74	100	98	6.43	96
Sieve no. 200 (%)	2	74.30	97	95	15.38	74

Taxonomic orders (percent)

Area: 92,931.26 km² (processing area)

Alfisols	Aridisols	Entisols	Histosols	Inceptisols	Mollisols	Spodosols	Ultisols	Vertisols
1.03	0.00	4.63	0.00	1.28	89.06	0.00	0.00	3.99

Tennessee

Area: 109,018.1 km² (shapefile feature)
          107,022.6 km² (processing area)

	MIN	MEAN	MAX	RANGE	STD	MEDIAN
Available water supply (cm)	5.91	21.75	40	34.09	7.36	22.92
Bulk density (g/cm)	0.15	1.45	1.75	1.6	0.07	1.47
Percent clay (<0.002 mm)	0.5	29.68	75	74.5	11.70	27.2
Forest productivity (ft³/ac/yr)	0	109.34	206	206	28.67	114
Kffact	0.02	0.36	0.78	0.76	0.08	0.37
Organic matter (% by weight)	0.01	0.71	95.08	95.07	0.93	0.49
Permeability (cm/hr)	1	14.45	122	121	14.53	9
pH	2.1	5.30	8	5.9	0.68	5
Rock depth (cm)	0	151.47	201	201	51.19	143
Sieve no. 10 (%)	10	80.23	100	90	18.04	87
Sieve no. 200 (%)	2	64.21	98	96	19.96	62

Taxonomic orders (percent)

Area: 107,305.70 km² (processing area)

Alfisols	Aridisols	Entisols	Histosols	Inceptisols	Mollisols	Spodosols	Ultisols	Vertisols
24.33	0.00	7.21	0.00	16.71	4.85	0.00	46.78	0.12

Texas*

Area: 394,937.9 km² (shapefile feature)
      380,819.6 km² (processing area)

	MIN	MEAN	MAX	RANGE	STD	MEDIAN
Available water supply (cm)	0.1	21.76	41.54	41.44	7.72	23.87
Bulk density (g/cm)	0.15	1.47	2.09	1.94	0.12	1.47
Percent clay (<0.002 mm)	0.3	35.47	77.5	77.2	13.63	36.2
Forest productivity (ft³/ac/yr)	0	88.80	200	200	46.60	100
Kffact	0.02	0.33	0.71	0.69	0.06	0.31
Organic matter (% by weight)	0.01	1.32	57.5	57.49	1.56	0.85
Permeability (cm/hr)	1	16.72	200	199	23.80	8
pH	2.1	7.06	9.1	7	1.08	7.5
Rock depth (cm)	18	140.43	201	183	61.54	127
Sieve no. 10 (%)	5	91.22	100	95	11.00	95
Sieve no. 200 (%)	1	64.76	99	98	19.49	67

Taxonomic orders (percent)
Area: 390,173.68 km² (processing area)

Alfisols	Aridisols	Entisols	Histosols	Inceptisols	Mollisols	Spodosols	Ultisols	Vertisols
32.94	2.38	5.31	0.03	7.13	27.41	0.01	7.26	17.53

Vermont

Area: 24,873.3 km² (shapefile feature)
      23,886.1 km² (processing area)

	MIN	MEAN	MAX	RANGE	STD	MEDIAN
Available water supply (cm)	8.45	17.39	56.28	47.83	3.89	16.74
Bulk density (g/cm)	0.23	1.57	2.02	1.79	0.18	1.63
Percent clay (<0.002 mm)	0.5	14.04	75	74.5	16.20	8
Forest productivity (ft³/ac/yr)	0	131.24	172	172	25.38	143
Kffact	0.02	0.45	0.78	0.76	0.10	0.43
Organic matter (% by weight)	0.05	10.98	93.25	93.2	17.13	5
Permeability (cm/hr)	1	42.41	390	389	48.80	22
pH	2.2	6.25	8.1	5.9	0.66	6.4
Rock depth (cm)	0	88.30	201	201	37.77	77
Sieve no. 10 (%)	2	79.48	100	98	10.90	80
Sieve no. 200 (%)	2	46.01	97	95	15.79	45

Taxonomic orders (percent)
Area: 24,187.72 km² (processing area)

Alfisols	Aridisols	Entisols	Histosols	Inceptisols	Mollisols	Spodosols	Ultisols	Vertisols
3.86	0.00	4.68	1.67	32.68	1.58	55.53	0.00	0.00

Virginia

Area: 103,134.0 km^2 (shapefile feature)
           101,353.8 km^2 (processing area)

	MIN	MEAN	MAX	RANGE	STD	MEDIAN
Available water supply (cm)	0.49	17.68	56.22	55.73	5.48	17.98
Bulk density (g/cm)	0.15	1.41	2.18	2.03	0.08	1.4
Percent clay (<0.002 mm)	0.5	28.57	68.8	68.3	12.67	25.5
Forest productivity (ft^3/ac/yr)	0	114.38	248	248	32.50	114
Kffact	0.02	0.34	0.76	0.74	0.09	0.31
Organic matter (% by weight)	0.01	1.22	65	64.99	4.53	0.46
Permeability (cm/hr)	1	21.63	299	298	19.67	13
pH	2.1	5.23	8	5.9	0.59	5.1
Rock depth (cm)	38	118.92	202	164	54.01	122
Sieve no. 10 (%)	2	82.71	100	98	17.93	90
Sieve no. 200 (%)	2	55.13	92	90	17.97	55

Taxonomic orders (percent)

Area: 102,188.92 km^2 (processing area)

Alfisols	Aridisols	Entisols	Histosols	Inceptisols	Mollisols	Spodosols	Ultisols	Vertisols
9.28	0.00	3.62	0.51	16.32	0.28	0.06	69.93	0.00

West Virginia

Area: 62,752.6 km^2 (shapefile feature)
           61,740.5 km^2 (processing area)

	MIN	MEAN	MAX	RANGE	STD	MEDIAN
Available water supply (cm)	6.06	13.91	33.88	27.82	4.25	13.54
Bulk density (g/cm)	0.15	1.39	2.02	1.87	0.07	1.4
Percent clay (<0.002 mm)	0.2	28.24	66	65.8	11.88	25.6
Forest productivity (ft^3/ac/yr)	0	104.94	211	211	36.24	100
Kffact	0.02	0.36	0.78	0.76	0.09	0.36
Organic matter (% by weight)	0.02	2.54	33.09	33.07	2.42	1.7
Permeability (cm/hr)	1	27.40	423	422	28.71	13
pH	2.1	5.36	8	5.9	0.75	5.3
Rock depth (cm)	25	106.02	202	177	32.72	102
Sieve no. 10 (%)	2	65.24	100	98	13.63	63
Sieve no. 200 (%)	7	49.68	92	85	16.05	49

Taxonomic orders (percent)

Area: 62,572.09 km^2 (processing area)

Alfisols	Aridisols	Entisols	Histosols	Inceptisols	Mollisols	Spodosols	Ultisols	Vertisols
15.40	0.00	3.65	0.01	24.21	0.39	0.27	56.06	0.00

Wisconsin

Area: 145,272.4 km² (shapefile feature)

141,878.8 km² (processing area)

	MIN	MEAN	MAX	RANGE	STD	MEDIAN
Available water supply (cm)	4.19	21.59	76	71.81	7.02	20.85
Bulk density (g/cm)	0.15	1.48	1.89	1.74	0.28	1.55
Percent clay (<0.002 mm)	0.3	15.40	69.5	69.2	11.89	11.3
Forest productivity (ft³/ac/yr)	0	57.80	200	200	21.84	55
Kffact	0.02	0.32	0.63	0.61	0.11	0.36
Organic matter (% by weight)	0.1	8.42	91.73	91.63	21.03	0.75
Permeability (cm/hr)	1	39.11	423	422	40.08	21
pH	2.2	6.18	8.1	5.9	0.76	6
Rock depth (cm)	0	146.71	201	201	59.04	201
Sieve no. 10 (%)	5	84.04	100	95	13.15	87
Sieve no. 200 (%)	2	50.70	100	98	26.56	50

Taxonomic orders (percent)

Area: 143,010.35 km² (processing area)

Alfisols	Aridisols	Entisols	Histosols	Inceptisols	Mollisols	Spodosols	Ultisols	Vertisols
37.91	0.00	10.79	8.03	6.18	14.30	22.79	0.00	0.00

APPENDIX 4: PYTHON SCRIPTS

The following scripts have been written for Python 2.5 and ArcGIX 9x to automate geoprocessing procedures needed to generate soil attribute raster grids. They do not require access to ArcInfo™ Workstation licensing. Within these scripts specific file paths are referencing locations of input and output folders. You will need to change these file paths to represent your local drive and folders. The first two scripts were written because the files were ready at different times due to the number of files being processed and the custom queries from the soil databases. Otherwise a single script could have been used. The third script (Generate County List) was created for use with the AML scripts (appendix 5), where the number of county files present in a state's folder is used to iterate through the processes. If you are processing many counties or states, it is advisable to run the AML scripts if you have access to ArcInfo Workstation. The computational time to produce the grid files will be reduced considerably.

Soil Join to Raster (soil_join2raster.py)

```python
# Import system modules
import sys, string, os, time, arcgisscripting

def printime():
    return time.strftime("%d/%m/%Y %H:%M:%S", time.localtime())

# capture the time at which the script is started at.
startime = time.time()

print 'Started script on: ', printime()

# Create the Geoprocessor object
gp = arcgisscripting.create()
gp.loghistory = False

# Load required toolboxes...
gp.AddToolbox("C:/Program Files/ArcGIS/ArcToolbox/Toolboxes/Conversion Tools.tbx")
gp.AddToolbox("C:/Program Files/ArcGIS/ArcToolbox/Toolboxes/Data Management Tools.tbx")

# Set the input workspace where the files to be processed are located
gp.Workspace = "C:\\Soil_Data\\gsmsoil_us\\" # Parent folder of the workspaces Eg:"E:\\STATE_DATASETS\\KY\\RASTER_DATA"

# define soil variables names
fprod = "Fprod"
sieve10 = "Sieve10"
sieve2 = "Sieve200"
tax = "taxonomic"
```

```
try:
    fcs = gp.ListFeatureClasses()
    fcs.reset()
    fc = fcs.next()

    while fc:
        shp = fc[0:3]
        fcLayer = shp+"_Layer"
        fprod_dbf = gp.Workspace + '\\' + shp + "_mapunit_fprod.dbf"
        sieve_dbf = gp.Workspace + '\\' + shp + "_mapunit_sieve.dbf"
        tax_dbf = gp.Workspace + '\\' + shp + "_mapunit_tax.dbf"
        tempout = gp.Workspace + '\\RASTER_DATA\\tempout'
        tempout2 = tempout + ".shp"
        fprod_field = shp + '_mapunit_fprod.FPROD_R'
        sieve10_field = shp + '_mapunit_sieve.SIEVENO10_'
        sieve2_field = shp + '_mapunit_sieve.SIEVENO200'
        tax_field = shp + '_mapunit_tax.TAXCODE'
        fprod_rf = shp + '_mapu'
        sieve10_rf = shp + '_mapu'
        sieve2_rf = shp + '_mapu'
        tax_rf = shp + '_mapu'
        raster_fprod = gp.Workspace + '\\RASTER_DATA\\Fprod\\' + shp + "_fprod"
        raster_sieve10 = gp.Workspace + '\\RASTER_DATA\\Sieve10\\' + shp + "_sieve10"
        raster_sieve2 = gp.Workspace + '\\RASTER_DATA\\Sieve200\\' + shp + "_sieve2"
        raster_tax = gp.Workspace+'\\RASTER_DATA\\Taxonomic\\' + shp + "_tax"

        gp.overwriteoutput = 1

        print "Making Feature Layer: " + shp, printime()
        # Process Forest Productivity (Fprod) soil variables
        # Process: Make Feature Layer...
        gp.MakeFeatureLayer_management(fc, fcLayer, "", "", "AREASYMBOL AREASYMBOL
VISIBLE;SPATIALVER SPATIALVER VISIBLE;MUSYM MUSYM VISIBLE;MUKEY MUKEY
VISIBLE")

        print "Add Join..." + shp, printime()
        # Process: Add Join...
        gp.AddJoin_management(fcLayer, "MUKEY", fprod_dbf, "MUKEY", "KEEP_ALL")

        print "Dissolving feature..." + shp, printime()
        # Process: Dissolve...
        gp.Dissolve_management(fcLayer, tempout, fprod_field, "", "MULTI_PART")

        print "Converting feature to raster..." + shp, printime()
        # Process: Feature to Raster...
```

```
gp.FeatureToRaster_conversion(tempout2, fprod_rf, raster_fprod, "30")
print shp+"Fprod is complete", printime()
print "------------------------------------"

print "Making Feature Layer: " + shp, printime()
# Process Sieve soil variables
# Process: Make Feature Layer...
gp.MakeFeatureLayer_management(fc, fcLayer, "", "", "AREASYMBOL AREASYMBOL
VISIBLE;SPATIALVER SPATIALVER VISIBLE;MUSYM MUSYM VISIBLE;MUKEY MUKEY
VISIBLE")

print "Add Join..." + shp, printime()
# Process: Add Join...
gp.AddJoin_management(fcLayer, "MUKEY", sieve_dbf, "MUKEY", "KEEP_ALL")

print "Dissolving feature..." + shp, printime()
# Process: Dissolve...
gp.Dissolve_management(fcLayer, tempout, sieve10_field, "", "MULTI_PART")

print "Converting feature to raster..." + shp, printime()
# Process: Feature to Raster...
gp.FeatureToRaster_conversion(tempout2, sieve10_rf, raster_sieve10, "30")

print "Dissolving feature..." + shp, printime()
# Process: Dissolve...
gp.Dissolve_management(fcLayer, tempout, sieve2_field, "", "MULTI_PART")

print "Converting feature to raster..." + shp, printime()
# Process: Feature to Raster...
gp.FeatureToRaster_conversion(tempout2, sieve2_rf, raster_sieve2, "30")
print shp+"Sieve is complete", printime()
print "------------------------------------"

print "Making Feature Layer " + shp, printime()
# Process Taxonomic soil variables
# Process: Make Feature Layer...
gp.MakeFeatureLayer_management(fc, fcLayer, "", "", "AREASYMBOL AREASYMBOL
VISIBLE;SPATIALVER SPATIALVER VISIBLE;MUSYM MUSYM VISIBLE;MUKEY MUKEY
VISIBLE")

print "Add Join..." + shp, printime()
# Process: Add Join...
gp.AddJoin_management(fcLayer, "MUKEY", tax_dbf, "MUKEY", "KEEP_ALL")

print "Dissolving feature..." + shp, printime()
# Process: Dissolve...
```

```
        gp.Dissolve_management(fcLayer, tempout, tax_field, "", "MULTI_PART")

        print "Converting feature to raster..." + shp, printime()
        # Process: Feature to Raster...
        gp.FeatureToRaster_conversion(tempout2, tax_rf, raster_tax, "30")
        print shp+"Tax is complete, moving to next file", printime()
        print "------------------------------------"

        fc = fcs.next()

except:
    gp.AddMessage(gp.GetMessages(2))
    print gp.GetMessages (2)
    print chr(7)
    print "Exited with Errors.... Something is wrong", printime()

# capture the time at which the script finishes.
endtime = time.time()
# calculate elapsed time.
etime = (endtime - startime)

# convert elapsed time into days, hours, minutes, seconds
def prntime(etime):
    s=etime
    m,s=divmod(s,60)
    h,m=divmod(m,60)
    d,h=divmod(h,24)
    return d,h,m,s
print 'Script has finished converting files time elapsed: (%d days %d hours %d minutes %d seconds'%
prntime(etime),')'
```

Soil to Raster (soil2raster.py)

```
# Import system modules
import sys, string, os, time, arcgisscripting

def printime():
    return time.strftime("%d/%m/%Y %H:%M:%S", time.localtime())

# capture the time at which the script is started at.
startime = time.time()

print 'Started script on: ',printime()

gp = arcgisscripting.create()
gp.loghistory = False
```

```
# Load required toolboxes...
gp.AddToolbox("C:/Program Files/ArcGIS/ArcToolbox/Toolboxes/Conversion Tools.tbx")
gp.AddToolbox("C:/Program Files/ArcGIS/ArcToolbox/Toolboxes/Data Management Tools.tbx")

#Set the input workspace where the files to be processed are located
gp.Workspace = "C:\\soil_data\\TN\\RASTER_DATA" # Parent folder of the workspaces Eg:"E:\\
STATE_DATASETS\\KY\\RASTER_DATA"

soilLst = ['AWS','Bulk_Density','Clay','Ksat','Organic_Matter','pH']

for soil in soilLst:
    print "Working on soil: " + soil + '...', printime()
    print "--------------------------------"

    #the workspace must be altered each time to reflect the different datasets
    inWorkspace = 'C:\\soil_data\\TN\\RASTER_DATA\\' + soil
    gp.Workspace = inWorkspace

    try:
        #List all feature classes and load the first one
        fcs = gp.ListFeatureClasses()
        #the reset command ensures that the first dataset is loaded properly
        #Loop through the list of features classes while performing the processes
        fcs.reset()
        fc = fcs.Next()

        while fc:
        #the print command can be replaced with any geoprocessing tool
        #and will be run on all feature classes within the Workspace

            tempfc = inWorkspace + "\\tempout"
            gp.overwriteoutput = 1

            rastername = fc[:-4]
            permout = inWorkspace + '\\' + rastername

            fldL = gp.ListFields(fc)
            fld = fldL.Next()
            nof=0
            while fld:
                fld = fldL.Next()
                nof = nof + 1
            fld = fldL.Reset()
            fld = fldL.Next()
            lno = 0
```

```
    while fld:
        if(lno==(nof-1)):
            fieldName = fld.Name
        lno = lno + 1
        fld = fldL.Next()


    fieldName = gp.ValidateFieldName(fieldName, os.path.dirname(fc))
    print "Starting to Dissolve ", fc, " on: ", fieldname + '... ', printime()
    #print "Dissolve out: "+tempfc


    gp.Dissolve_management(fc, tempfc, fieldName, "", "MULTI_PART")


    print "Converting dissolved features to raster based on field: ", fieldname + '... ', printime()
    tempfc2 = tempfc + '.shp'
    gp.FeatureToRaster_conversion(tempfc2, fieldName, permout, "30")
    print "Raster Output: " + permout + '... ', printime()
    print "--------------------"


    fc = fcs.next()


except:
    gp.AddMessage(gp.GetMessages(2))
    print gp.GetMessages (2)
    print "Exited with Errors.... Something is wrong!",printime()


soilLst2 = ['KFFACT']


for soil in soilLst2:
    print "Working on soil: "+soil+'...',printime()
    print "-----------------------------------"


    #the workspace must be altered each time to reflect the different datasets
    inWorkspace = 'C:\\soil_data\\TN\\RASTER_DATA'+'\\'+soil
    gp.Workspace = inWorkspace


    try:
        #List all feature classes and load the first one
        fcs = gp.ListFeatureClasses()
        #the reset command ensures that the first dataset is loaded properly
        #Loop through the list of features classes while performing the processes
        fcs.reset()
        fc = fcs.Next()


    while fc:
        #the print command can be replaced with any geoprocessing tool
```

```
#and will be run on all feature classes within the Workspace

    # Process: Add Field...
    print "Starting to Add Field...KFFACT"
    gp.AddField_management(fc, "KFFACT", "FLOAT", "", "", "", "", "NON_NULLABLE",
"NON_REQUIRED", "")

    # Process: Calculate Field...
    print "Calculating Field values"
    gp.CalculateField_management(fc, "KFFACT", "[KfactRF]", "VB", "")

    tempfc = inWorkspace + "\\tempout"
    gp.overwriteoutput = 1


    rastername = fc[:-4]
    permout = inWorkspace + '\\' + rastername

    fldL = gp.ListFields(fc)
    fld = fldL.Next()
    nof=0
    while fld:
        fld = fldL.Next()
        nof = nof + 1
    fld = fldL.Reset()
    fld = fldL.Next()
    lno = 0
    while fld:
        if(lno==(nof-1)):
            fieldName = fld.Name
        lno = lno + 1
        fld = fldL.Next()

    fieldName = gp.ValidateFieldName(fieldName, os.path.dirname(fc))
    print "Starting to Dissolve ", fc, " on: ", fieldname + '... ', printime()
    gp.Dissolve_management(fc, tempfc, fieldName, "", "MULTI_PART")

    print "Converting dissolved features to raster based on field: ", fieldname + '... ', printime()
    tempfc2 = tempfc + '.shp'
    gp.FeatureToRaster_conversion(tempfc2, fieldName, permout, "30")
    print "Raster Output: " + permout + '... ', printime()
    print "-------------------"

    fc = fcs.next()
```

```
except:
    gp.AddMessage(gp.GetMessages(2))
    print gp.GetMessages (2)
    print "Exited with Errors.... Something is wrong!", printime()


soilLst3 = ['RockDep']
# ['RockDep']


for soil in soilLst3:
    print "Working on soil: " + soil + '...', printime()
    print "----------------------------------"

    #the workspace must be altered each time to reflect the different datasets
    inWorkspace = 'C:\\SOIL_DATA\\TX\\RASTER_DATA\\' + soil
    gp.Workspace = inWorkspace

    try:
        #List all feature classes and load the first one
        fcs = gp.ListFeatureClasses()
        #the reset command ensures that the first dataset is loaded properly
        #Loop through the list of features classes while preforming the processes
        fcs.reset()
        fc = fcs.Next()

        while fc:
        #the print command can be replaced with any geoprocessing tool
        #and will be run on all feature classes within the Workspace

            tempfc = inWorkspace + "\\tempout"
            rastername = fc[:-4]
            permout = inWorkspace + '\\' + rastername
            gp.overwriteoutput = 1

            fldL = gp.ListFields(fc)
            fld = fldL.Next()
            nof=0
            while fld:
                fld = fldL.Next()
                nof = nof + 1
            fld = fldL.Reset()
            fld = fldL.Next()
            lno = 0
            while fld:
                if(lno==(nof-1)):
```

```
        fieldName = fld.Name
      lno = lno + 1
      fld = fldL.Next()

    fieldName = gp.ValidateFieldName(fieldName, os.path.dirname(fc))
    print "Starting to Dissolve ", fc, " on: ", fieldName + '... ', printime()
    gp.Dissolve_management(fc, tempfc, fieldName, "", "MULTI_PART")

    print "Converting dissolved features to raster based on field: ", fieldName + '... ', printime()
    tempfc2 = tempfc + '.shp'
    gp.FeatureToRaster_conversion(tempfc2, fieldName, permout, "30")
    print "Raster Output: " + permout + ' ... ', printime()
    print "--------------------"

    fc = fcs.next()
  except:
    gp.AddMessage(gp.GetMessages(2))
    print gp.GetMessages (2)
    print "Exited with Errors.... Something is wrong!", printime()

# capture the time at which the script finishes.
endtime = time.time()
# calculate elapsed time.
etime = (endtime - startime)

# convert elapsed time into days, hours, minutes, seconds
def prntime(etime):
  s=etime
  m,s=divmod(s,60)
  h,m=divmod(m,60)
  d,h=divmod(h,24)
  return d,h,m,s
print 'Script has finished converting files time elapsed: (%d days %d hours %d minutes %d seconds'%
prntime(etime),)'
```

Generate County List (genCountyList.py)

```
# This script is used to generate a list of county soil shapefiles to inform
# the soil2rast.aml and the soil_join2rast.aml
#
# Import system modules
import sys, string, os, time, arcgisscripting

# setup  timer
def printime():
  return time.strftime("%d/%m/%Y %H:%M:%S", time.localtime())
```

```python
# capture the time at which the script is started.
startime = time.time()

print 'Started script on: ',printime()

# Create the Geoprocessor object
gp = arcgisscripting.create()
gp.loghistory = False

# Set workspace and generate a list of county names from shapefiles.
gp.Workspace = "C:\\GIS_DATA\\NRCS_SOILS\\AL" #"C:\\soil_data\\MN\\RASTER_DATA\\
Bulk_Density"
fcs = gp.ListFeatureClasses("", "POLYGON")

# create file to contain the county list
print "openning file"
fh = open('C:\\GIS_DATA\\NRCS_SOILS\\AL\\RASTER_DATA\\countysoil.txt', 'a')

fc = fcs.next()

while fc != "":
    print >>fh, fc[0:5]
    fc = fcs.next()

print "county list created"
fh.close()

# capture the time at which the script finishes.
endtime = time.time()
# calculate elapsed time.
etime = (endtime - startime)

# convert elapsed time into days, hours, minutes, seconds
def prntime(etime):
    s=etime
    m,s=divmod(s,60)
    h,m=divmod(m,60)
    d,h=divmod(h,24)
    return d,h,m,s
print 'Script has finished converting files time elapsed: (%d days %d hours %d minutes %d seconds'%
prntime(etime),')'
```

APPENDIX 5: ARC™ MACRO LANGUAGE SCRIPT

The following two scripts have been written for ArcInfo™ Workstation 9.3 to convert vector coverages to raster grids. Within these scripts, specific file paths are referencing locations of input and output folders. These will need to be changed to represent your local drive and folders. Due to the number of files being processed and the custom queries from the soil databases, two scripts were written because the files were ready at different times; otherwise a single script could have been used. These scripts were developed from the original Python code provided in appendix 4 to speed up the computational time. These AMLs cannot be used alone; rather they are designed to speed up a portion of the Python scripts that took many hours to run, conversion to a raster. Therefore they are intended to be run after running either soil_dissolve.py or soil_join2dissolve.py (included on the CD-ROM), which converts the shapefiles to a coverage file.

Soil Coverages to Raster (soil2rast.aml)

```
/* 04/09/2010
/* To convert soil coverages to grid
/*
/* This aml reads all the records in a file sequentially
/* and does something on them
&args fil
/* if error, continue anyway
 &severity &error &ignore

&ab &off
&if [null %fil%] &then &ret Usage: &r soil2rast.aml C:\ SOIL_DATA\TX\RASTER_DATA\
countysoil.txt
&if ^ [exists %fil%] &then &ret NOTE: %fil% Does NOT exist!
&sv unit = [open %fil% opens -r]
&if %opens% = 0 &then &do
  &sv rec = [read %unit% reads]
   &do &while %reads% = 0
     /* Do something with the record
     &type %rec%

     /* AWS
     &workspace ..
     &workspace C:\SOIL_DATA\TX\RASTER_DATA\AWS
     polygrid %rec%_aws_d %rec%_aws AWS150  /* polygrid(<in_cover> <out_grid> {value_item}
{lookup_table} {weight_table})
     30   /* cell size
     y   /* convert entire coverage

     /* Bulk Density
     &workspace C:\SOIL_DATA\TX\RASTER_DATA\Bulk_Density
     polygrid %rec%_bd_d %rec%_bd DB3RDBAR  /* polygrid(<in_cover> <out_grid> {value_item}
{lookup_table} {weight_table})
```

```
30   /* cell size

y   /* convert entire coverage


/* Clay

&workspace ..

&workspace C:\SOIL_DATA\TX\RASTER_DATA\Clay

polygrid %rec%_clay_d %rec%_clay Clay  /* polygrid(<in_cover> <out_grid> {value_item}
{lookup_table} {weight_table})

30   /* cell size

y   /* convert entire coverage


/* KFFACT

&workspace ..

&workspace C:\SOIL_DATA\TX\RASTER_DATA\KFFACT

polygrid %rec%_kffac_d %rec%_kffact KFFACT  /* polygrid(<in_cover> <out_grid> {value_
item} {lookup_table} {weight_table})

30   /* cell size

y   /* convert entire coverage


/* Ksat

&workspace ..

&workspace C:\SOIL_DATA\TX\RASTER_DATA\Ksat

polygrid %rec%_ksat_d %rec%_ksat Ksat  /* polygrid(<in_cover> <out_grid> {value_item}
{lookup_table} {weight_table})

30   /* cell size

y   /* convert entire coverage


/* Organic Matter

&workspace ..

&workspace C:\SOIL_DATA\TX\RASTER_DATA\Organic_Matter

polygrid %rec%_om_d %rec%_om OrgMatter  /* polygrid(<in_cover> <out_grid> {value_item}
{lookup_table} {weight_table})

30   /* cell size

y   /* convert entire coverage


/* pH

&workspace ..

&workspace C:\SOIL_DATA\TX\RASTER_DATA\pH

polygrid %rec%_ph_d %rec%_ph pHwater  /* polygrid(<in_cover> <out_grid> {value_item}
{lookup_table} {weight_table})

30   /* cell size

y   /* convert entire coverage


/* Rock Depth

&workspace ..

&workspace C:\SOIL_DATA\TX\RASTER_DATA\RockDep
```

```
        polygrid %rec%_rock_d %rec%_rockdep Dep2ResLyr  /* polygrid(<in_cover> <out_grid>
{value_item} {lookup_table} {weight_table})
        30   /* cell size
        y   /* convert entire coverage

        &sv rec = [read %unit% reads]
      &end
&end
&S close [close %unit%]
&ab &on
&call stop
&ret
/* **********************************************
&routine stop
&ab &on
&S closed [close -all]
&ab &off
&stop
&RET


/* **********************************************
```

Soil Join to Raster (join2rast.aml)

```
/* 04/09/2010
/* To convert soil coverages to grid
/*
/* This aml reads all the records in a file sequentially
/* and does something on them
&args fil
/* if error, continue anyway
 &severity &error &ignore

&ab &off
&if [null %fil%] &then &ret Usage: &r join2rast.aml C:\SOIL_DATA\TX\RASTER_DATA\
countysoil.txt
&if ^ [exists %fil%] &then &ret NOTE: %fil% Does NOT exist!
&sv unit = [open %fil% opens -r]
&if %opens% = 0 &then &do
  &sv rec = [read %unit% reads]
    &do &while %reads% = 0
      /* Do something with the record
      &type %rec%
       /* Forest Productivity
      &workspace C:\SOIL_DATA\TX\RASTER_DATA\Fprod
```

```
    polygrid %rec%_fprod_d %rec%_fprod %rec%_mapu  /* polygrid(<in_cover> <out_grid>
{value_item} {lookup_table} {weight_table})
        30   /* cell size
        y    /* convert entire coverage


        /* Sieve10
        &workspace ..
        &workspace C:\SOIL_DATA\TX\RASTER_DATA\Sieve10
        polygrid %rec%_sie1_d %rec%_sieve1 %rec%_mapu  /* polygrid(<in_cover> <out_grid> {value_
item} {lookup_table} {weight_table})
        30   /* cell size
        y    /* convert entire coverage


        /* Sieve200
        &workspace ..
        &workspace C:\SOIL_DATA\TX\RASTER_DATA\Sieve200
        polygrid %rec%_sie2_d %rec%_sieve2 %rec%_mapu  /* polygrid(<in_cover> <out_grid> {value_
item} {lookup_table} {weight_table})
        30   /* cell size
        y    /* convert entire coverage


        /* Taxonomic Order
        &workspace ..
        &workspace C:\SOIL_DATA\TX\RASTER_DATA\Taxonomic
        polygrid %rec%_tax_d %rec%_tax %rec%_mapu  /* polygrid(<in_cover> <out_grid> {value_
item} {lookup_table} {weight_table})
        30   /* cell size
        y    /* convert entire coverage


    &sv rec = [read %unit% reads]
    &end
&end
&S close [close %unit%]
&ab &on
&call stop
&ret
/* *************************************************
&routine stop
&ab &on
&S closed [close -all]
&ab &off
&stop
&RET


/* *************************************************
```

APPENDIX 6: R STATISTICAL SOFTWARE CODE

The following code has been written for R 2.12.2 to add a field (TAXCODE) to a data frame, assign a corresponding numeric value to a taxonomic order, and export the records to a DBF file. The following code is provided for two cases: (1) the soil data have been exported from the Access database in DBF format or (2) the data are in XLS format. If you are converting data from the XLS format to DBF, installation of Perl is required.

```
#####################
# For .dbf files    #
#####################

# load required libraries
library("base")
library("boot")
library("foreign") # write to .dbf

# sets the working directory
setwd("C:/SOIL_DATA/IN/RASTER_DATA/IN_Join")

# assign files in working directory to variable 'fld'
fld <- list.files(getwd(), pattern = "*_tax")

# assigns the TAXCODE to the TAXORDER values
soil <- data.frame(TAXORDER = c('Alfisols', 'Aridisols', 'Entisols', 'Histosols', 'Inceptisols', 'Mollisols', 'Spodosols', 'Ultisols', 'Vertisols'), TAXCODE = c(1,2,3,4,5,6,7,8,9))

# loop throught files in directory
for(i in fld) {

# reads in values from a .dbf file
doc <- data.frame(read.dbf(i))

# add dummy values to new column
doc$TAXCODE <- 0

# match the soil file to the doc file
doc$TAXCODE <- match(doc$TAXORDER, soil$TAXORDER, nomatch = 0)

# writes to new file
write.dbf(doc, file = strtrim(i, 18))
}

#####################
# For .XLS files    #
#####################
```

```
# REQUIRES PERL TO BE INSTALLED

# load required libraries
library("base")
library("boot")
library("foreign") # write to .dbf
library("gdata") # reading .xls files

# sets the working directory
setwd("C:/SOIL_DATA/NE/RASTER_DATA/IN_Join")

# assign files in working directory to variable 'fld'
fld <- list.files(getwd(), pattern = "*_tax")

# assigns the TAXCODE to the TAXORDER values
soil <- data.frame(TAXORDER = c('Alfisols', 'Aridisols', 'Entisols', 'Histosols', 'Inceptisols', 'Mollisols',
'Spodosols', 'Ultisols', 'Vertisols'), TAXCODE = c(1,2,3,4,5,6,7,8,9))

# loop throught files in directory
for(i in fld) {

# reads in values from a file .xls
doc <- data.frame(read.xls(i, sheet=1, perl="C:/Perl/bin/perl.exe"))

# add dummy values to new column
doc$TAXCODE <- 0

# match the soil file to the doc file. Because the soil file has classes = to the row numbers
# you can just use the matched row id and assign to the doc file.  If there is no match then it
# gets a class of 0.
doc$TAXCODE <- match(doc$taxorder, soil$TAXORDER, nomatch = 0)

# writes to new file
write.dbf(doc, file = strtrim(i,18))
}

#############################################
# convert fprod from .xls to .dbf

fld <- list.files(getwd(), pattern = "*_fprod")
for(i in fld) {
doc <- data.frame(read.xls(i, sheet=1, perl="C:/Perl/bin/perl.exe"))
write.dbf(doc, file = strtrim(i,19))
}
```

```
##########################################
# convert sieve from .xls to .dbf

fld <- list.files(getwd(), pattern = "*_sieve")
for(i in fld) {
doc <- data.frame(read.xls(i, sheet=1, perl="C:/Perl/bin/perl.exe"))
write.dbf(doc, file = strtrim(i,19))
}
```

Peters, Matthew P.; Iverson, Louis R.; Prasad, Anantha M.; Matthews, Steve N. 2013. **Integrating fine-scale soil data into species distribution models: preparing Soil Survey Geographic (SSURGO) data from multiple counties.** Gen. Tech. Rep. NRS-122. Newtown Square, PA: U.S. Department of Agriculture, Forest Service, Northern Research Station. 70 p.

Fine-scale soil (SSURGO) data were processed at the county level for 37 states within the eastern United States, initially for use as predictor variables in a species distribution model called DISTRIB II. Values from county polygon files converted into a continuous 30-m raster grid were aggregated to 4-km cells and integrated with other environmental and site condition values for use in the DISTRIB II model. In an effort to improve the prediction accuracy of DISTRIB II over our earlier version of DISTRIB, fine-scale soil attributes replaced those derived from coarse-scale soil (STATSGO) data. The methods used to prepare and process the SSURGO data are described and geoprocessing scripts are provided.

KEY WORDS: habitat suitability, raster aggregation, Soil Data Viewer, geographic information system, eastern United States

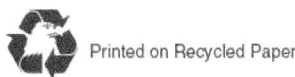

Northern Research Station

www.nrs.fs.fed.us